MARK SHATTUCK

THE HIDDEN PATH OF ADVERSITY

DISCOVER GOD'S 7 UNEXPECTED SECRETS
TO GIVE YOU THE DESIRES OF YOUR HEART
THROUGH HARDSHIP AND PAIN

TABLE OF CONTENTS

I NEVER EXPECTED TO WRITE THIS BOOK

"I don't think the way you think.
The way you work isn't the way I work.
For as the sky soars high above earth,
so the way I work surpasses the way you work,
and the way I think is beyond the way you think."

ISAIAH 55:8 (The Message)

In June of 2009, my family and I were down to our last $700 — that was all we had! The housing market collapse had wiped us out.

I wasn't supposed to be in such a desperate situation. You see, in 2002, I opened my very own residential design firm, achieving great success designing multi-million-dollar custom homes. I graduated from one of the top architecture schools in the country, and worked hard in the housing industry learning how to be a great architect. So, when I opened my own firm, I was ready to succeed.

And I did — phenomenally! But what I didn't know was that my architecture firm was built on a ticking time bomb. The housing market "bubble" was growing every year into a monster that would soon cost Americans almost $10 trillion dollars of their wealth. The housing and credit market collapse was the worst financial crisis since the Great Depression — and the longest! And my little firm was right in its path.

So, in 2008, when Bear Stearns collapsed, I lost 60 percent of my business in just one month due to massive economic fear and uncertainty across the entire US. Only five months later, Lehman Brothers also collapsed, causing me to lose 90% of my business before the end of that year.

I was in complete panic mode! I could see everything slipping away faster than I could do anything about it. I lived with a daily sense of dread as I desperately tried to find work. It was like I had a large weight on my shoulders that just kept getting heavier and heavier. Most people I knew in my industry were going bankrupt all around me. They were losing all their money, losing their businesses, losing their homes — even their marriages were being destroyed because of this nightmare!

So, when I was down to my last $700, it was game over for my family and I. That's when I couldn't pay the mortgage to keep our home. I couldn't pay for my family to have medical care. We barely had enough money for food! How could this have happened? We were at the end of the road, and my family and I were about to be financially destroyed. But …

God was up to something that I didn't have eyes to see — yet.

You see, I have always sought God with everything I've got — as best as I knew how. And so, as this crisis was crashing down on us, I went to God for help and direction. *Turns out, that's exactly what He wants us to do* — but for some very unexpected reasons, which I will reveal in this book.

So while I was in full panic mode, God was just waiting for me to let Him come through for us! And He did! He started doing and revealing things I never could've imagined. In my darkest hour of the housing market collapse, God started bringing me more business than I had ever secured — and none of it was seed I had sown! He saved us with ***miracle architecture deals*** — like manna in the housing market wilderness. It was amazing!

But the best part of it all was that God was teaching me how to find a hidden path in the midst of my adversity. It turns out there's ***a hidden path*** in everyone's adversity. There's a hidden path in yours too. It's the path to abundant Life. It's what Jesus said He came to give us:

> *"I came that they may have life, and have it abundantly."*

JOHN 10:10

That's great news — sign me up! I've always wanted the abundant Life Jesus promised. In fact, I've searched for it more than anything else in life. And the older I get, the more I want it. I also ache for what Jesus offers in Matthew 11:28-30:

> *"Are you tired? Worn out? Burned out on religion? Come to me. Get away with me and you'll recover your life. I'll show you how to take a real rest. Keep company with me and you'll learn to live freely and lightly."*

JESUS (The Message)

Live "free and light?" Heck yeah, I want that! I'll bet you want it too. Don't we all? Yet being tethered to a world where success and

There's a hidden path in everyone's adversity. There's a hidden path in yours too. It's the path to abundant Life.

contentment aren't guaranteed no matter how hard we attempt to achieve them can make this unbelievable offer seem just that — unbelievable. But I can tell you *it's real!*

I spent decades on the same never-ending treadmill you're probably on right now. You know the one where you chase after expectations and outcomes that always seem just out of reach, never truly delivering what you really want, even if you get them. How about we leave that toilsome path behind and find the path to abundant Life instead — the one Jesus promised more than 2,000 years ago?

But before we jump into that, here's a little bit about me, and where we're headed in this book. My quest to discover this elusive treasure started at a very early age. As a child of missionary parents, my life began immersed in Christianity — in a good way (it can get a bit twisted up for some). My mother led me to Christ as my Lord and Savior while sitting on the blue and white tile floor of our home in the Dominican Republic when I was just three years old. It's the earliest memory I have to this day. And even as a young child, I remember being intrigued by God's promise of abundant Life. It created a desire in me to discover it for myself.

But no matter how "good" I lived, the prize of happiness and peace remained out of reach. And as an adult, no matter how successful I became, security and validation were frustratingly fleeting. Yet, the treadmill of life's expectations didn't slow down or stop — it just kept speeding up on me!

Then, something big happened in my journey — adversity! Fourteen long years of it and counting (not just the housing market collapse)! Despite all my efforts to find abundant Life, I was suddenly thrust into the exact opposite experience I was seeking. I couldn't believe it! These difficult circumstances wracked me with confusion and frustration. Yet my adversity drove me to take a deeper look at the Bible to see what God had to say about my undesirable circumstances. My relentless search revealed how adversity is a consistent (and *necessary*) part of God's work in the lives of His followers.

Wait! Did I just say adversity is necessary? Yes, I did — but don't panic. Adversity is not God's desire for our lives — *abundant Life is!* However, as we'll discover throughout this book, adversity is the best way for God to lead us to the abundant Life He promised. You see, through all my adversity, God led me to the fulfillment of my truest desires. And He continues to bless me with His goodness beyond my expectations to this day, even though adversity also remains a constant. It's part of life, whether we like it or not.

And so, I want you to have that same Life-giving relationship with God — He longs for that as well. He's been saying it for thousands of years. We just haven't been able to hear it. I know I wasn't! But God can do unexpected things with adversity — if we let Him:

> *"I'm taking her back into the wilderness ... I'll turn Heartbreak Valley into Acres of Hope."*
>
> **HOSEA 2:14** (The Message)

Now, if the idea of necessary adversity upsets you, well, you're in good company. I'm not happy about it, and neither is God. It's certainly not how He intended things to be. But in my own adversity, here's a secret I discovered to be true: that the very thing we desire the most — abundant Life, Life to the full — can only be found through the necessary work of adversity.

You see, **I never intended to write this book** because adversity was never part of my "life equation." But now it is. I've discovered that adversity is actually the "fast track" to finding the very thing we desire the most. The life-changing realities of my adversity have given me a passion to help those struggling as I have, to discover a new path — to discover the hidden path to abundant Life. That's why I've written this book, after all.

In this book I'll reveal:

- why adversity is required to gain abundant Life
- how to make it through the wilderness of adversity
- and, how God gives us the desires of our heart — *abundantly!*

God's core desire is to see His creation living abundantly happy, peaceful, secure, loved, and meaningful lives. It's always been His desire, and always will be. He never changes. So, take heart! That which you desire the most is what God has for you. But because of one massive disconnect in us all (which I get to straight away in chapter one), the path to abundant Life is far different than we think. That's why Jesus said few find it.

Will you journey with me — into the wilderness of adversity — to discover this hidden path, and find the Life you were created for?

I can't promise you it will be easy. In fact, there will be times when it will be very difficult to accept what's in this book. But I can guarantee that if you stay with me — *and* do the necessary "heart work" — you will find this hidden path, and the abundant Life you were born to live. Are you ready? Then let's go!

God's desire is to
bless His creation.

But something in us
stands in His way
(and it's not our sin).

HOLD THE PRESS!

Just as this book was about to go to print, all hell broke loose across the world with the coronavirus pandemic! Now, more people than ever are facing intense adversity. And due to a 10,000-point stock market sell-off in one month (March 2020), my architecture business was decimated — *again!*

But this time, something's different. I'm different. I'm not afraid. I'm not panicking. I have a new understanding — a new way of living — that has no need for fear and insecurity.

While I certainly don't like what's happening to the world — to America — I must admit, I like this *new way* of living by faith instead of by sight. I have no idea how it's going to pan out, but I do know that God has something unimaginably good for me — because that's His core desire. I'm walking through this next wilderness with a whole new perspective — that's Life-giving.

I hope you find it too!

> *"I pray that the eyes of your heart may be enlightened, so that you will know what is the hope of His calling, what are the riches of the glory of His inheritance in the saints, and what is the surpassing greatness of His power toward us who believe."*

EPHESIANS 1:18-19 (NASB)

CHAPTER 1

THE GREATEST THING IN LIFE — WHICH SO FEW FIND

WHAT EVERYONE WANTS

God's desire is to bless His creation. This is revealed from the first page of the Scriptures to the last. One of the most famous verses in the Bible establishes God's blessing intentions:

> *"For I know the plans I have for you," declares the Lord, "plans to prosper you and not to harm you, plans to give you hope and a future."*

JEREMIAH 29:11 (NIV)

And it's not just this one verse! There's plenty of evidence in scripture to reveal God's desire to bless His children. It's the underlying point of all the Bible stories of Abraham and David, Joseph and the Israelites, Esther, and Daniel, just to name a few. Their stories reveal how God is ready and willing to bless those who seek His Life-giving passion. In fact, one of the main reasons God tells us about the Israelites in the Old Testament is to show us that He has a *Promised Land* for all who are willing to believe in

Him and receive the great good He is ready to give His children. It's really true!

In fact, King David — who went through his share of adversity — makes an amazing claim on God's behalf:

> *"Delight yourself in the Lord and He will give you the desires of your heart."*

PSALMS 37:4 (NASB)

How can this be in the Bible — you know, God's book — if it's untrue? In fact, Jesus' promise in John 10:10 is the greatest offer of all time ever made by anyone:

> *"I came that they may have life, and have it abundantly."*

You see, we all want abundant Life. It's what every human being is looking for every day of their lives. The good news is that God wants it for us too — it's what He created us for in the first place. It's what Jesus said He came down from heaven to give us. But along with the promise of this amazing offer, Jesus gave us a terrifying warning about this quest for Life:

> *"Enter through the narrow gate; for the gate is wide and the way is broad that leads to destruction, and there are many who enter through it. For the gate is small and the way is narrow that leads to life, and there are few who find it."*

MATTHEW 7:13–14 (NASB)

To be clear, these verses aren't speaking about salvation. They're referring to Life as God intended for us. Salvation had to happen first, in order for the promise of abundant Life to be available to those who are redeemed from darkness. Without salvation, a person cannot receive abundant Life because it's incompatible with their nature and identity. It's like mixing water and oil, dark and light. It won't happen.

Abundant Life is the state of being fully satisfied and content through God's Life-giving power because it's His nature and identity to do so. That's why Jesus said He came to give it to us. Why would He say this otherwise? Yet most Christians seem to have a devastating disconnect regarding this promise. I've found that all Christians believe without hesitation in the salvation proclamation of John 3:16, yet few equally believe in the availability of abundant Life offered by Jesus in John 10:10. Why is that?

I think the disconnect that keeps so many from finding the path to true Life *is unbelief.* This can be a tough pill to swallow for Christians. After all, don't we have to believe to be a "believer?" We do, but it's a little more complicated than that. We all have a whole pile of misbeliefs and unbeliefs which blind us from the very thing we desire the most — abundant Life.

Abundant Life is the state of being fully satisfied and content through God's Life-giving power because it's His nature and identity to do so. That's why Jesus said He came to give it to us. Why would He say this otherwise?

So, let me ask some hard questions here. Why do so few Christians find the path to abundant Life? Why do so few — if any at all — receive the desires of their heart? Why do most wander in a never-ending wilderness of discontent rather than thrive in the promised land God has for them? Why is it that most people find themselves desperately trying to fill an underlying emptiness, but never succeed?

The truth is, we all live with some degree of discontent every day of our lives. Yet, even though we are doing everything we can to minimize this reality, it never works. No matter how morally or hedonistically a person lives, discontentment is always present.

Here's what that means for me: if I take an honest look beyond the busyness of my life, I see an underlying longing in my heart; a discontentedness that's with me all the time. It drives me to find satisfaction in work, more money, fun experiences, and enjoyable relationships. But nothing seems to resolve the ache. Nothing sticks. Does that sound familiar? Jesus referred to our discontent as the thirst and hunger of our hearts — which He came to satisfy.

> *"I am the bread of life; he who comes to Me will not hunger, and he who believes in Me will never thirst."*

JOHN 6:35 (NASB)

Whoa, wait a minute! Never thirst? Not hunger? Again, sign me up! Isn't that what we all want — to satisfy that nagging hunger and thirst in our hearts? To scratch the proverbial itch?

So, what are we missing then, that keeps us from this unbelievable reality? What are we doing wrong that makes life feel more like a wilderness of insatiable thirst than a promise land of abundant Life?

THE REQUIREMENT OF ADVERSITY

To answer that, we need to come face to face with another startling reality hidden in God's scriptures. It's not good news like the wonderful promise of abundant Life. There's another reality about God that is a requirement to find and walk the path to true Life. It's this: God always leads His people into wilderness experiences *before* they can enter their promised land of abundant Life. Every story and every character in the Bible had great adversity at its core. Though each path they walked was different, all were orchestrated by God. Your story is no different. Everyone who wants to enjoy abundant Life must first journey through the wilderness of adversity in order to remove the obstacles that keep us from it. Moses had to remind the Israelites of this unsettling reality:

> *"Remember how the Lord led you into the wilderness … causing you to hunger…"*

DEUTERONOMY 8:2–3 (NIV)

As much as we'd like to avoid adversity, it's a requirement to finding the path that leads to the abundant Life God offers. Life's wildernesses of adversity are painful and confusing places. They include frightening scarcity — even soul-crushing tragedy. And discovering that God has led us into this place of adversity, to cause us to hunger in it, is too much for most to bear.

The wilderness of adversity becomes the breaking point where many give up on a God who inflicts His own with hunger like Moses revealed God did to His chosen people. It's a place that causes us to cry out to God, and yet it's the place He often seems to be most silent and unresponsive. Even the strongest of believers are brought to their knees in the wilderness.

David described this well in Psalm 107:23-27 (TNIV):

> *"Some went out on the sea in ships; they were merchants on the mighty waters. They saw the works of the LORD, His wonderful deeds in the deep.*
>
> *"**For He spoke and stirred up a tempest** that lifted high the waves. They mounted up to the heavens and went down to the depths; in their peril their courage melted away. They reeled and staggered like drunkards; they were at their wits' end ..."*

A Shot of Hope!

Are you feeling dismayed by what I'm saying? Maybe even tempted to close this book? I completely understand! Like I said, this was never the book I thought I'd write. But stay with me on this journey, because I promise you it gets better — much better! We just have to get through the wilderness first.

It'll be worth it — I promise!

Why would a loving God deliberately require His children to endure adversity? More so, why would *He* stir up tempests in our lives? Why would *He* lead us into a wilderness and cause us to hunger, as Moses tells us God did to His chosen people? There's a reason for it all. You see, adversity is a spiritual "chemotherapy

God always leads His people into wilderness experiences — adversity — before they can enter their promised land of abundant Life.

regimen" intended to remove the deadly cancer of our natural ways of seeing and living life. Here's what this means:

During my adversities, I dove deep into the Bible, desperately seeking answers and revelation. The Holy Spirit led me to many helpful passages and stories, but throughout the rest of Deuteronomy chapter 8 I discovered some unexpected ways God works in hardship and pain. In this powerful chapter Moses reveals God's intentions for leading the Israelites into the hardships of the wilderness. I found seven reasons hidden in Deuteronomy 8 that reveal God's purposes for bringing such trials and difficulties into the lives of His children. *They tell of an unseen path which, if followed, will lead us to our promised land and give us the desires of our heart.*

The next seven chapters will unpack these seven reasons Moses revealed to the Israelites for why God led them into the wilderness and caused them to hunger. We'll dig into seven key phrases that reveal the obstacles to entering the promised land God has for those who are His children.

To state the obvious, it's our natural tendency to avoid adversity. But God knows something we're blind to: no matter how godly we may try to live, our natural human condition has us fixated on a path that leads to destruction — a path of self-sufficiency and self-reliance that is in opposition to the abundant Life Jesus came to give us. Adversity creates the opportunity to heal this devastating condition which infects all of us. Adversity, it turns out, is the antidote and "GPS" to finding the abundant Life God has for us. Remember, God's greatest desire is to bless His children with full and abundant Life. This is His greatest desire for you right now. Will you trust that He knows what He's doing to get you there? He can, if you'll let Him!

Everyone who wants to enjoy abundant Life must first journey through the wilderness of adversity in order to remove the obstacles that keep us from it.

MY BACK-TO-BACK ADVERSITIES

As I mentioned briefly in the introduction, in 2002 I began the great adventure of self-employment by opening my own residential architecture firm. I had six years of architecture school under my belt, plus eight years of experience working for several prestigious residential design firms in Atlanta, Georgia. But I was oblivious to the ground work that had already been laid for the worst housing and credit markets collapse since the Great Depression. By 2005, the housing market was growing fast, which meant I was doing very well. By 2007, I made more money in one year than I had imagined I'd make. I was on my way to becoming a millionaire!

However, by the spring of 2008, the housing market "bubble" burst! And like everyone else in my industry, I leaped into action to find work. I immediately increased my marketing efforts to find new deals. Nothing happened. I then took a risk by creating an expensive new marketing book of house plans to help find potential clients. Again, nothing worked. In fact, nothing was

Adversity, it turns out, is the antidote and "GPS" to finding the abundant Life God has for us now.

working for anyone else in the industry either. And so, by the dark winter days of 2008, I had lost 90% of my business. At that point, the housing market was officially in a Depression and there was no work to be found. I couldn't believe the wonderful career I had chosen and worked so hard to build had become a devastating financial wilderness. Most of the people, businesses, and developments I knew in the industry — who were much more successful than I — were going bankrupt on a monthly basis. It was terrifying!

By June of 2009, my worst fears became reality. My family and I were down to our last $700. I was so full of fear and anxiety, not knowing how I would pay the bills. My wife Kim and I (with our two young children) feared we would lose our home. It seemed our number was finally up to join the ranks of bankruptcies happening all around us.

But we didn't! God came through in miraculous ways! Similar to the Israelites who needed food to survive their wilderness journey, God gave us financial "manna" all the way from 2009 to 2012 to make it through the Great Recession. And just like the manna God gave the Israelites, ours was "just enough" to survive. This made those four long years a hair-raising rollercoaster ride of frightening scarcity mixed with heavenly provision. Though God showed up, I allowed the wasteland of the housing market to grip me with the daily fear that all would be lost at any moment.

By 2013, the housing market was recovering. I was slowly beginning to secure enough design projects to make ends meet for several months out. And by 2014, the housing market was really heating up. The nightmare was finally over! Or so I thought...

You see, God did not create the worldwide economic collapse that dragged me and my family into that financial wilderness. That mess was created by a mix of destructive government policies and greedy investment strategies. But in 2014, God "stirred up a tempest" in my life, like David described in Psalm 107, and I was plunged into another financial wilderness. This time, it was caused by two custom home builders who had been bringing me the majority of my work in the housing market recovery. Coincidentally though, they both joined a builder services group expanding out of Florida that had its own in-house architectural design center. This meant my services were no longer needed, and in a matter of a couple months, I lost 90% of my business — all over again!

You're probably thinking, *"No big deal, Mark. The housing market is back to normal now. Just go get new clients."* Yeah, I thought the same thing. I ramped up my marketing and networking efforts, expecting to find new clients in a now fast-growing housing industry. But things took an unexpected turn. I couldn't secure a single new client no matter how hard I tried! It was so strange and out of character for me because I knew how to make deals happen. Yet suddenly, I couldn't. Everyone else I knew in the industry was going gangbusters by now — except me. Then it dawned on me: God wasn't allowing me to make deals happen!

Yes, God was thwarting me. He was disrupting my ability to get new business to such a degree that this second financial wilderness was *worse* than the 2008 to 2012 recession! I kid you not. And so, I quickly fell back into fear and anxiety. I couldn't believe this was happening again! This time I even became clinically depressed (which was a first for me). I had longed for the days when the terrifying housing market depression would be over — and it was — but now God had brought me back into the same nightmare.

I want to be clear that our financial troubles were not created by mistakes or bad decisions we made. Kim and I were not living lavishly, nor spending our money in foolish ways. Our reality was that in both of these financial wildernesses, I struggled deeply to bring in a consistent stream of paying work due to circumstances beyond my control or influence. In both cases, God had a hidden path for us to walk by faith and not by sight. So, as we progress through this book, I'll share more about the amazing things God had in store for us.

And so, this second financial wilderness — our "Recession 2.0," as I'll call it — would last another four agonizing years. But God added another challenge to this second trial: He became excruciatingly silent. I cried out to God with more intensity and frequency than ever before, but He remained silent. I did everything I could to hear from God to get clarity and direction in this dark and painful place. He still remained silent. I struggled deeply to understand why God would do this, especially when I needed His revelation now more than ever. King David struggled with God's silence as well. He said:

> *"Why, LORD, do you stand far off? Why do you hide yourself in times of trouble?"*

Psalms 10:1 (NIV)

My natural reaction was to think I was doing something wrong, or not doing something right. There are many stories in the Bible of godly people wondering the same thing in their adversity. The best example is Job, who desperately cried out to God to understand what he had done to cause the unthinkable tragedy thrust upon him. He and his three friends spent 37 chapters trying to figure out what he did to deserve his misfortune. Yet the reasons any of us experience adversity and loss are far beyond our natural understanding.

I would eventually discover that God was up to something far deeper than I expected, and far greater than I could imagine in my adversity. Even His silence was part of His plan to change me into someone new — to transform me into His child who is able to receive abundant Life.

The first reason so few find the path to abundant Life is because we don't see adversity correctly. It's *un*natural for us to consider that the opposite experience of abundant Life *is the path to it*. Therefore, few Christians give themselves over to the transformational work of adversity. Instead, they run from it.

It was through my transformation in adversity that I discovered the Life-giving power of the seven secrets hidden in Deuteronomy 8. They reveal God's *"treasures of darkness, riches stored in secret places,"* as the prophet described in Isaiah 45:3 (TNIV).

If you're willing, you too can discover this rarely found path to abundant Life. But there are obstacles to finding it, and they're much more difficult to remove than we naturally think. Nevertheless, let's start this journey toward this greatest-of-all prizes. Our roadmap for this quest will be Deuteronomy 8:2-18 (TNIV).

The wilderness of adversity is the God-given opportunity to give up on our futile quests to find happiness, peace, and security apart from Him.

"Remember how the LORD your God led you all the way in the wilderness these forty years, to humble and test you in order to know what was in your heart, whether or not you would keep his commands. He humbled you, causing you to hunger and then feeding you with manna, which neither you nor your ancestors had known, to teach you that people do not live on bread alone but on every word that comes from the mouth of the LORD.

"Your clothes did not wear out and your feet did not swell during these forty years. Know then in your heart that as a man disciplines his son, so the LORD your God disciplines you.Observe the commands of the LORD your God, walking in obedience to him and revering him. For the LORD your God is bringing you into a good land—a land with streams and pools of water, with springs flowing in the valleys and hills; a land with wheat and barley, vines and fig trees, pomegranates, olive oil and honey; a land where bread will not be scarce and you will lack nothing; a land where the rocks are iron and you can dig copper out of the hills.

"When you have eaten and are satisfied, praise the LORD your God for the good land he has given you. Be careful that you do not forget the LORD your God, failing to observe his commands, his laws and his decrees that I am giving you this day. Otherwise, when you eat and are satisfied, when you build fine houses and settle down and when your herds and flocks grow large and your silver and gold increase and all you have is multiplied, then your heart will become proud and you will forget the LORD your God, who brought you out of Egypt, out of the land of slavery.

"He led you through the vast and dreadful wilderness, that thirsty and waterless land, with its venomous snakes and scorpions. He brought you water out of hard rock. He gave you manna to eat in the wilderness, something your ancestors had never known, to humble and test you so that in the end it might go well with you. You may say to yourself, 'My power and the strength of my hands have produced this wealth for me.' But remember the LORD your God, for it is he who gives you the ability to produce wealth, and so confirms his covenant, which he swore to your ancestors, as it is today."

CHAPTER 2

SECRET #1: OUR GREATEST OBSTACLE TO FINDING LIFE

"...to humble you..."

DEUTERONOMY 8:2-3 (NIV)

WE HAVE A BIG PROBLEM

*T*he first thing God is up to in our adversity is to give us an exceedingly deep "reality check" regarding our ability to secure happiness on our own. He knows we need to come to the realization that we are powerless in our efforts to get what we're really after. We must recognize that we are fully dependent on Him for the thing we desire and need the most — abundant Life.

No matter how hard we try to find abundant Life by our own means, we won't succeed. No matter how successful we may become in this life, we cannot gain what we truly desire.

Jesus stated our condition very clearly in John 6:53 (NASB):

"… you have no life in yourselves."

Jesus is revealing that the *Life* we so desperately seek is not in us. It can only come from God. Yet the thirst of our heart creates such intrinsically rooted commitments to finding Life apart from God, that we miss His path to it. This drives us to find it in anything we can. Therefore, in order to receive the good that God has for us, we must first be humbled with difficult circumstances which reveal our complete inability to secure what we desire most. The wilderness of adversity is the God-given opportunity to give up on our futile quests to find happiness, peace, and security apart from Him. This was true for me. In fact, adversity was exactly what I needed in order to discover abundant Life — in spite of my own efforts.

SATISFACTION "UNDER THE SUN"

God knows we have a big problem that is far more severe than we can imagine. As Jesus said, we lack true Life, which leaves our heart insatiably hungry and thirsty. Regardless of how we live, we can't secure Life on our own. Ultimately, we all become enslaved to the things we seek to satisfy us here "under the sun."

Now, these three words — *under the sun* — reveal a vital clue to our struggle to find true Life. They define the realm we live in — the realm we're trapped in. The book of Ecclesiastes repeats these words over and over revealing a powerful secret to our reality here under the sun, which we've all refused to acknowledge. They reveal why our efforts to find Life are so futile. The writer of Ecclesiastes says:

> *"I have seen all the works which have been done under the sun, and behold, all is vanity and striving after the wind."*

ECCLESIASTES 1:14 (NASB)

Here's what's so important about this strange verse. The word "vanity" means *vapor or breath,* which means *fleeting and futility.* Some Biblical translations use the word "meaningless," which is a bit misleading because not everything under the sun is meaningless. My children aren't meaningless. Churches and orphanages aren't meaningless. So, the proper view to understand our daily existence as expressed throughout Ecclesiastes should be as follows, according to the literal definitions of the Biblical wording:

> *"Everything under the sun is a vapor and a breath, fleeting and futile, a chasing after the wind."*

Let me explain why this is so critically important to our quest for Life. These three words "under the sun" represent the realm in which we seek happiness, peace, security, meaning and purpose in everything we do. It includes going to school, working, playing, raising a family, going to church, and volunteering for good causes. It refers to the realm of human activity — both good or bad — in which we are trying to find happiness.

What we don't recognize is that true Life cannot be found in anything under the sun, because nothing under the sun has Life to give. This means that the abundant Life we seek — the Life God made us for — is not found in anything under the sun. Yet we are all intensely driven by the thirst in our souls to find something that will finally make us happy — that will finally quench our thirst. But what we seek *cannot be found under the sun.* That's why Jesus said so few find it.

Therefore, God's first purpose for leading us into a wilderness of scarcity and adversity is to give us the opportunity (and it's just that, an opportunity) to discover the Life-changing revelation of Ecclesiastes, that *everything under the sun is fleeting and futile* — that nothing under the sun has the ability to give us what we're after, which is abundant Life.

Take a moment to allow this reality to sink in: that nothing under the sun has Life to give. It never has. It never will.

Until we get this, we will miss God's intentions for creating us in the first place. Just because sin has horrendously altered our human reality, God is still after His original intention of being our Life source apart from anything here under the sun. Yet, we are far more deceived by our human reality than we could ever imagine without the transformation opportunity that hardship and pain gives us. Those who understand this will find the path to Life Jesus revealed.

Another Shot of Hope!

God's desire is that all His children live the abundant Life He made them to possess! But He won't violate our free will. Therefore, God must use adversity to conform our thinking and actions to His Life-giving ways. We're headed there in this book. We just have to get through some tough stuff first.

Don't give up! The good stuff is coming!

True Life cannot be found in anything under the sun, because nothing under the sun has Life to give.

Abundant Life — as God intended from the beginning of creation — is to be fully happy, secure, at peace, loved, validated, having meaning and healthy relationships, without lack or fear of loss.

WHAT ARE WE *REALLY* AFTER?

So, what is this thing called Life — abundant Life — we are so desperately seeking? What is it we're *really* after in life, after all? The word "Life" in this book, and in Jesus' promises, isn't about breath in our lungs or a pulse in our heart. It's the Greek word "Zoe" which means:

"Absolute fullness of life; life that is active, vigorous, and blessed."

NEW AMERICAN STANDARD GREEK LEXICON

More specifically, *"Zoe"* is the following seven core needs we **_all_** thirst for and chase after every day of our lives. These are the underlying ingredients that form the abundant Life we so desire — that God made us for. Our seven core needs are:

Happiness (joy, satisfaction)

Security (both physical and financial)

Peace (being at rest, free of worry)

Love (feeling accepted, wanted, chosen)

Validation (success, value, respect)

Meaning (purpose, fulfillment)

Relationships (friendship, companionship)

These are the most fundamental human needs. All the things we do in life are simply means to these ends. And we seek them so intensely because God created us to have these core needs fully met at all times, without ever losing or lacking them at all. Yet, we were born without them due to the brokenness of this world, which created the thirst we've lived with everyday since.

Here's an amplified definition of Abundant Life — as God intended from the beginning of creation: it is to be fully happy, secure, at peace, loved, validated, having meaning and life-giving relationships, without lack or fear of loss. If this sounds unrealistic and idealistic, it's because it's completely unnatural to our human reality. It *is*, however, fully real and available in God's reality. He made us to be filled with these seven core values the moment he created mankind. It was a fundamental reality in His creation intention. It remains His desire for us now.

But due to sin, we've become misled to find Life through things apart from God. And since all our natural human efforts are a vapor and a breath — a chasing after the wind — they don't work. Even for those who are able to gain great wealth, success, and power, which gives them the ability to do whatever they want, these seven core needs are never truly met. That's because nothing under the sun has the ability to actually fulfill these needs. *Nothing under the sun gives Life because nothing under the sun has Life to give. Only God does.*

We certainly experience life-giving moments and seasons, but they are always fleeting. Our soul simply ends up thirsty again. Even if a person lives with authentic godly intentions and purposes, they will still be fundamentally discontent. Great vacations or charitable acts may feel good (and rightly so) — for a while — but the reality of life under the sun is that satisfaction and contentment *always dissipate*. No matter what we possess or do, we eventually come back to "Lifelessness" again.

"There is a way which seems right to a man, but its end is the way of death."

PROVERBS 14:12 (NASB)

This death is living without the "Zoe-life" God created us for — that Jesus came down from heaven to give us. And so, the first thing we must learn in the wilderness of adversity is that this realm we live in — here under the sun — can never give us what we truly desire, what we need the most. Until we suffer loss, we will keep believing we can get Life from better outcomes, pleasant circumstances, and positive results in this world. Loss gives us the opportunity to release our fixation on finding Life under the sun. The wilderness of loss and adversity is God's way of bringing us to the point of realizing we will never find what we're looking for here under the sun. This is humbling, to say the least. However, we must come to our senses about our condition. We must learn a new way of seeing Life *in our adversity.*

Loss gives us the opportunity to release our fixation on finding Life under the sun.

COMING TO OUR SENSES

In the parable of the Prodigal Son, Jesus revealed the transformational power of adversity our heavenly Father is after in our lives:

> *"The young man became so hungry that even the pods he was feeding the pigs looked good to him. But no one gave him anything. When he finally came to his senses, he said to himself, 'At home even the hired servants have food enough to spare, and here I am dying of hunger!'"*

LUKE 15:16-17 (NLT)

God's goal in adversity is not to humiliate us, or "put us in our place." That's not the kind of humility He's after. Rather, *God wants our discontentedness to bring us to our senses.* For the prodigal son, this came as he found himself having squandered his inheritance, and eating less than pigs. Through this parable, Jesus reveals that in this place of deep and painful hunger, the wayward son came to his senses to return to his father, who had abundance available all the while.

Jesus gave us this story for a reason — it describes all of us! No matter how successful we may become, our hearts and souls are starving for fulfillment because we were not created to "feed on the pods" of this world. Until we come to our senses and realize that only our good Father has what we need, we are in danger of continuing to try to make something work here under the sun. Therefore, God must use the wilderness of adversity as a humbling reality check to bring us to our senses — if we are willing to accept His work in it.

To be clear, "feeding on the pods" of this world consists of far more than blatant sinful living. It includes all the normal human activities and things we pursue in which to find satisfaction and fulfillment.   Most often, it centers on our jobs, money, and relationships to generate feelings of happiness, peace, and security. Our heavenly Father longs for us to come to our senses that these natural things cannot give us what He created us for. Here's what this looked like in my story.

COMING TO *MY* SENSES

It took me 10 years of severe financial adversity to finally begin to understand that nothing under the sun could make me happy, give me peace and security, or make me feel validated as a man. God stripped away some of the most important things in my life that I was using to satisfy the thirsty places in my heart — specifically my need for security and validation through success in my work. Though I was as committed to godly living and biblical teaching as I knew how, I was still expecting to find a certain level of contentment in this life through *better outcomes, pleasant circumstances, and positive results*. We all do this every second of our lives. This is natural for us to do.

But God knew that success under the sun would rob me of discovering the fullness of true Life *only He can give*. So, He led me into a financial wilderness and caused me to hunger in ways that would give me the opportunity to surrender to His hidden path to true Life.

I must admit though, for the majority of the 10 years of my adversity, I had no clue what He was up to. I didn't think there was a deeper purpose in all my troubles. I was simply trying to survive. The only thing I was focused on was finding the quickest way out of my financial adversity so I could get back to some level of normalcy, and ultimately, a sense of peace and security again. And so, I desperately sought better outcomes through my own wisdom and efforts.

I believe this is why God activated the "second round" of financial adversity in my life after the Great Recession of 2008-2012 was over — my Recession 2.0, as I call it. Though I had done a pretty good job of living by faith through the housing market depression (albeit with a massive amount of fear and anxiety), I was still believing in the comfort of better outcomes and pleasant circumstances once the recession ended. God knew I hadn't moved from self-reliance to full surrender yet. He knew I hadn't come to my senses yet about what I was feeding on for Life.

I needed to recognize the complete and utter futility of my own wisdom and strategies in order to see God's greater good *beyond* better outcomes and pleasant circumstances. So, He had to take me deeper into a frightening wilderness of financial adversity a second time.

The intensity of this next adversity humbled me by revealing how little control I had to arrange for my own happiness, peace, and security. It showed me how easy it was for pleasant circumstances to quickly turn into a nightmare, no matter how hard I worked. Again, it took me 10 years of adversity to finally come to my senses to understand that I was completely incapable of securing the very thing I was seeking — which was security and validation in Jesus Christ instead of success through my work.

The wilderness of loss and adversity is God's way of bringing us to the point of realizing we will never find what we're looking for here under the sun.

It's imperative that we all come to the humbling reality that we are completely powerless to secure what we desire the most through our own efforts and wisdom. This is God's first goal in our transformation through adversity. Just like Moses revealed to the Israelites, this is God's first purpose for leading us into a wilderness and causing us to hunger in it. This isn't what God intended for His creation. But in His great love for us, He will not violate our free will, and force us to come to Him the right way. And so, He leverages the scarcity and pain of the hardships and tragedies of our broken reality to give us the opportunity to come to our senses — to come to Him for the Life we desire.

Remember, God is *for* us, not against us. We must keep seeking His presence in our adversity, believing He is up to something we can't yet see. We must believe He is ultimately good, even though our circumstances may not feel like it. The next secret takes us further down this hidden path, to reveal what we're really living for.

CHAPTER 3

SECRET #2: WHAT ARE YOU REALLY LIVING FOR?

"...to test you..."

DEUTERONOMY 8:2 (NIV)

OUR HIDDEN SOURCES

God's second purpose for bringing us into the wilderness and causing us to hunger, is to test our commitments. God's test in adversity is specifically designed to show us what we are *truly living for*. It's a straight-forward test: are we committed to living fully for God and His unseen reality, or are we committed to satisfying our thirst through outcomes here under the sun?

Loss and adversity quickly expose what we are living for. Our false supports for Life are revealed through our emotional reaction toward loss. Our intensifying thirst in the wilderness exposes the

Loss and adversity
quickly expose what
we are living for.

Our intensifying thirst
in the wilderness
exposes the natural
things we have fixated
our hopes on for Life.

natural things on which we have fixated our hopes for Life. When my business and finances collapsed, I was terrified I would lose everything I had worked so hard for, rather than fearlessly believe God's desire was to rescue me as He promises all throughout His scriptures. The housing market collapse revealed that my trust for security was in this industry under the sun, rather than in God alone. The problem is, almost everyone thinks this way about their job security too. But God's passion has always been for His creation to trust *in Him alone* for Life, rather than in created things.

Let God's own words reveal how broken our self-sufficiency is in this powerful rebuke:

> *"My people have committed two sins: They have forsaken me, the spring of living water, and have dug their own cisterns, broken cisterns that cannot hold water."*

JEREMIAH 2:13 (NIV)

Until we accept the reality that nothing under the sun will ever give us the Life we truly and desperately need, we will not see how self-reliant we are. As God clearly reveals in this verse, the essence of sin is to seek Life from anything other than God alone. Adversity and pain can reveal the reality of our "broken cisterns" hidden in our hearts. If we are willing to admit our self-sufficiency, the ball is in our court to repent, even when we believe we've been diligently living for God. Repentance is a wonderful way to experience God's love for us, for He is quick to forgive and redeem those who come to Him in sincere surrender. Until then, God must use hardship and pain to get us there.

This testing is deeply confusing for those who are living for God as well as they know how. The testing breaks us so deeply because we struggle to believe such painful and tragic tests are necessary.

God seems overbearing — even cruel — to allow such extreme adversity in our lives. Isaiah 55:8-9 reminds us that God's ways are not our ways, and His thoughts are not our thoughts. In our adversity, we must accept we have a *very* limited understanding of God.

In one of his many letters to believers, Paul further warns us that:

> *"... a natural man does not accept the things of the Spirit of God, for they are foolishness to him; and he cannot understand them ..."*

1 CORINTHIANS 2:14 (NASB)

We must understand that our reality here under the sun is a battle between our flesh and our spirit. Our flesh is this "natural man" that Paul says cannot understand nor accept God's ways. These natural ways of the flesh still remain in all of us beyond salvation. Even the most committed believer still has far more natural tendencies than he or she would like to believe. And so, God will expose these natural beliefs and strategies — sometimes with fierce adversity — to give us the opportunity to come to a willingness for Life-giving repentance. This is one of the most powerful, yet most avoided, aspects of sanctification. In the wilderness of adversity, the hunger God may bring upon us will be so out of line with our natural ways that we will often consider God's ways as foolish. In other words, He will do things we would not do if we had His power and resources.

This will test our views and beliefs about God Himself. In fact, God may bring such painful adversity into our lives that our incomplete beliefs about Him will be violated, like Job and his friends experienced. Many suffering believers have come to the point of questioning if God even exists. God's purpose in this

God will expose our natural beliefs and strategies — sometimes with fierce adversity — to give us the opportunity to come to a willingness for Life-giving repentance.

crucible of belief is not only to test our commitment to Him, but to remove the many false beliefs about Him we've unwittingly accumulated throughout our life.

The Bible is clear that God did shocking things to His chosen people — even to His own son! Every character in the Bible experienced deep adversity in some way or another. As I experienced my own, I came to realize that God was personally responsible for a lot of it. This hadn't been part of my understanding of God. Then I found this unexpected verse in which God clarifies the source of the calamity the Israelites — His chosen people — were experiencing. This verse shows how serious God is about adversity being necessary to bring us to the Life He created us for:

> *"I am the LORD, and there is no other; I form the light and create darkness, I make peace and create calamity; I, the LORD, do all these things."*

ISAIAH 45:6-7 (NKJV)

Yes, this is in the Bible! These are God's own words. In fact, notice how many times God insists *He's responsible* for forming darkness and creating calamity. According to the definitions of the word "calamity" used here, God is telling us in no uncertain terms, that He creates adversity, trouble, disaster, and harm!

I don't know about you, but I didn't sign up for that when I became a Christian! I signed up for the "light and prosperity" part, but certainly not the "darkness and calamity." This reveals the most fundamental test of God's work in our lives: will we still believe and trust that He is *ultimately good* in the face of darkness and calamity He allows, or even brings upon us?

This doesn't align with our human nature. It's foolishness to us! *"This can't be God's will!"* we cry out in the midst of our trouble and darkness. I did, many times! And so, we must gain a correct understanding that God really does "bring darkness and calamity" on His children, not just on "the wicked," as we've likely compartmentalized. Only then will we be able to see how this unexpected reality of God's testing — this foolishness to our natural thinking — is actually part of His abundant Life plan for us. We must realize and accept that His testing through adversity has a Life-giving purpose.

Again, Job is the best example of this terrifying biblical reality. It's important to realize that Job is pronounced righteous by God in the first chapter and the last, meaning he had done nothing wrong to deserve his affliction. Rather, it was an "all-in-poker-style" bet between God and Satan to see if Job would pass the test of ultimate adversity. But God included some great news at the end of that crazy story, to reveal His goodness:

> *"The LORD blessed the latter part of Job's life more than the former part."*

> **JOB 42:12** (TNIV)

Another Shot of Hope

Yes, the Isaiah passage that God creates calamity is one of the scariest verses in the Bible! But wishing it to be untrue won't change anything. We must believe **God is good** even when He does things we believe are bad. He's up to something far beyond our understanding. The Bible is clear on this. So, stay with me — it will be worth it!

THE "FOOLISH" PATH OF ADVERSITY

Like Job, when God tests our commitments, it will hurt. It will be hard. It will feel like foolishness for us to stay and endure it. In fact, everything in us will cry, *"Get out of this situation! Do whatever it takes to make the pain go away!"* I wrestled deeply with thoughts like these throughout my adversity. But I discovered something vital in those desperate moments: that we must determine if God's intention is for us to stay in the wilderness. If so, then to remove ourselves from our adversity (if we are able) may establish a compromise with our flesh, which leads to death. In the midst of God's testing, staying put in our adversity is most often the only path to true Life. Exiting the trial by our own wisdom and arrangements will only disqualify us from discovering the abundant Life we so desperately desire.

There are three tests we must use in order to determine if God is calling us to remain in our adversity:

TEST #1: We must hear from God

Since God's ways are so different from ours, the possibility that our adversity has been ordained by God must be confirmed by Him. Without hearing God's voice, we will never find the hidden path to abundant Life, and never gain our heart's true desires.

Remember, the foundation of this book is based on Moses's statement to the Israelites that it was God who led them into the wilderness, and it was God who caused them to hunger. Since this is so unnatural to us, we must seek His confirmation in our wilderness experience to see if God has a greater purpose in our hardship and pain.

I had to hear God's words, because everything in me wanted relief. And so, Chapter 4 is entirely dedicated to our crucial need to hear God's Life-giving words, both through His scriptures and from His Holy Spirit. So, there's much more on this coming up.

TEST #2: We must receive wise counsel

No one can accomplish God's intentions for their life on their own because God has created us for community. And the confusion and desperation that comes with adversity means we need wise counsel more than ever. But we must be very careful and discerning in selecting who gives us this important counsel. There are few who understand God's "foolish" ways and can help us see beyond our pain and confusion in order to stay the course, if that's what God has for us.

Job's three friends were not wise counselors to him. They kept insisting he'd done something evil to deserve his affliction. And so, God rebuked them severely in the end. Therefore, we must be very shrewd in selecting those we allow to counsel us.

TEST #3: We must develop a discerning heart

The final test, after hearing from God and the counsel of wise and experienced believers, is to recognize the truth the Holy Spirit is revealing *in our hearts*. But this takes deep maturity and discernment. It requires looking past our natural desperation to get out of adversity, in order to perceive the invitation of God to

In the midst of God's testing, staying put in our adversity is most often the only path to true Life.

Exiting the trial by our own wisdom and arrangements will only disqualify us from discovering the abundant Life we so desperately desire.

remain in the trial of our wilderness. Developing a discerning heart is a long and dedicated journey of maturity and growth. It requires seeking God and His reality more than anything else in life. It requires the deep and intentional practice of the "four streams" of spiritual living: discipleship, counseling, healing, and spiritual warfare. (The details of these practices are beyond the teachings in this book, but others — like the powerful works of John Eldridge — have done a great job of expanding on them, which I highly recommend.)

Joseph's example

I believe this struggle of staying in our God-ordained wilderness versus exiting our adversity (again, for those who have the option) is best exemplified in the amazing story of Joseph in the book of Genesis (chapters 37 through 41). Joseph goes from being his father's favorite son, to being sold as a slave by his jealous brothers. He ends up as a slave to an Egyptian Captain named Potiphar. This was Joseph's worst nightmare! It was the complete opposite reality of his favored life back home. It was also completely opposite of the visions of greatness given to him by God. Yet God was with Joseph *in* his adversity by blessing everything he did — as a slave! The same thing happened when he was falsely accused of raping Potiphar's wife and thrown into prison. Now his situation went from bad to worse! Again, as Joseph's adversity intensified, God was with Joseph by blessing everything he did, even in prison. Here's what the Bible tells us was the reality of Joseph's character in his 14-year-long adversity:

> *"So, Potiphar left everything he had in Joseph's care; with Joseph in charge, he did not concern himself with anything except the food he ate."*

GENESIS 39:6 (TNIV)

"The warden paid no attention to anything under Joseph's care, because the Lord was with Joseph and gave him success in whatever he did."

GENESIS 39:23 (TNIV)

In light of these two verses, I believe Joseph had the means and control of his environment to escape his undeserved adversity. In both cases, I believe he could have easily planned his escape and return home to the comfort and love of his homeland. He had every opportunity to run, but he didn't. I believe Joseph sensed God had a greater purpose in it all, even though David would later reveal how Joseph's adversity was deeply painful and confusing to him. David said about Joseph:

"They humbled his feet in fetters [shackles]; the iron pierced his soul."

PSALM 105:18 (DOUAY-RHEIMS)

God is always up to something, even when it feels like He's not. Again, His ways are not our ways. His thoughts are not our thoughts. When we view our circumstances through our natural wisdom, God's ways will seem like foolishness. *Again, He most often won't do things the way we would if we had His power and resources.* If God directs us to remain in our adversity, we must trust that His ways are better than our ways. We must surrender in belief that He has a greater good in store for us. In fact, the following verses reveal God's intensity about staying in our adversity when He directs us to do so:

"Let those who walk in the dark, who have no light, trust in the name of the Lord and rely on their God. But now, all you who light fires and provide yourselves with flaming torches, go, walk in the light

of your fires and of the torches you have set ablaze. This is what you shall receive from My hand: You will lie down in torment."

ISAIAH 50:10-11 (TNIV)

This may seem like an extremely harsh response from God, but He has a completely different purpose in our darkness than we naturally care to consider. Our natural instincts in adversity are always to reduce or remove the painful situations in our lives. We naturally "light our own torches" as an attempt to find a path out of our hardship. I believe that most of the time God is asking us to sit still in the darkness of our adversity. He's testing to see if we will trust Him and seek Him to bring about His unknown outcomes. This will feel like foolishness to us! But notice the consequences for those who are unwilling to rely on God in the midst of such dark places. God warns: "You will lie down in torment!" This is the result of living a life separated from God's Life-giving reality, even if you are a believer. Torment is the ultimate consequence of putting our hope in better outcomes, pleasant circumstances, and positive results under the sun.

A "FOOLISH" TEST FROM GOD

Here's a powerful example of God's testing in Exodus that I found to be intensely frustrating. God's heavy-handedness in this test seemed wrong to me, yet I believe God does this in every adversity:

> *"Then Moses led Israel from the Red Sea, and they went out into the wilderness ... they went three days in the wilderness and found no water ... and there [the LORD] tested them."*

EXODUS 15:22 & 25 (NASB)

This passage is the very next move of God after the epic miracle of the parting of the Red Sea and the destruction of the Israelite's mortal enemies, the Egyptian army. Because of what they had just witnessed, the Israelites were on cloud nine. They were as happy as they could be. God had just saved them in epic form before their very eyes.

Yet, God then led them into the wilderness, taking them on a route which had no water for three days into the journey. We must put ourselves in their place to feel their frightening reality. This was a desperate situation! The Israelites were about two million people in total and could never carry enough water to make it past three days without finding a spring or pond along the way. By day three, they were panicking. There was no possible source of water as far as the eye could see. They became confused. They began to suspect God was not really intent on helping them after all. In verse 24, they began complaining to Moses about God, essentially saying, "Did God lead us this far, part the sea, destroy our enemy, to then forget where to find water for us?"

But here's where God's ways go from confusing to down right offensive in this story. At the end of the third day, as the Israelites were feeling death's grip, they cried out to God for help. God then led them to a pool of water. They're saved! Or so they thought. The fastest runners reached the pool first, scooping up a desperate mouthful of water to quench their agonizing thirst, only to discover that the pool is bitter! God's oasis of salvation is actually sulfur-laced water that burns their throats!

They gasp with ever-increasing thirst. They stagger in confusion. They cry out to God again. They have no other options as death comes closer and closer. God then instructs them to throw a branch of dead wood into the bitter pool. Really? That's God's solution? Is this another joke? Yet, someone humors God and throws the lifeless wood into the undrinkable water. It suddenly becomes sweet — and life-giving.

I think it's no coincidence that the word "bitter" in this passage (Exodus 15:23) means "discontented." This reveals God's requirement that we taste the discontentment of everything under the sun, even if we are following God through the wilderness with all the faith we have in us. God then requires us to wait — rest — right where we are, until He transforms the discontent and bitterness or our own ways of living into sweet Living Water.

There are many similar (and baffling) stories throughout the Bible. Stories of God doing things we would *never* do to those we claim to love. These stories show us that God will test our view of Him and His ways, often through mind-boggling circumstances. In fact, most of the time, God doesn't leverage His power and resources the way we think He should. God's hidden path in the wilderness of adversity is to cause us to taste the bitter lifelessness of this world, no matter how faithfully we may be living.

Likewise, in our wilderness of loss and scarcity, God tests our beliefs. He leads us into the wilderness of adversity and causes us to hunger in order to give us the opportunity to see the object of our trust and belief — Him, or better circumstances. In my adversity, I discovered a deeply rooted reality in my heart. I had to recognize that all my life my fundamental trust was in better outcomes, pleasant circumstances, and positive results. I was only able to see this broken commitment so deeply buried in my heart as the result of my adversity. Had I focused only on resolving or removing my pain, I would have entirely missed God's intentions

Most people fail God's test of adversity because they do not know how to see the purpose of the wilderness God has led them into.

for my good. Paul reveals this unnatural reality of pain in his second letter to the Corinthian church.

"For the sorrow that is according to the will of God produces a repentance without regret, leading to salvation ..."

2 Corinthians 7:10 (NASB)

RESTING IN OUR WILDERNESS

One of the most difficult tests in our wilderness will be God's call for us to rest in our adversity. This is much more than accepting to remain in our hardship by giving up our efforts to exit our undesirable circumstances, if we are able. It's quite amazing to realize how God instituted a full day of rest upon the Israelites *while they were in the wilderness!* And God was so serious about this humanly unthinkable requirement, that He even caused His miracle of ongoing manna to rest on the seventh day. You see, it's natural to believe that one would never rest from survival while in a wilderness of scarcity — unless God is with you. And that was God's point. He withheld His supernatural provision in order to test their faith *in Him* rather than in what ever security they could gather and store in their own strengths and abilities.

"It is a day of sabbath rest, and you must deny yourselves ..."

Leviticus 16:31 (NIV)

As we walk our path of adversity, we must discern how to perceive God's call to rest in Him at all times. We must learn to deny our natural tendencies to activate our strengths and wisdom to arrange for better outcomes. Until we learn God's way of surrender in adversity, we will never find the rest our souls so desperately desire, as God warned in Hebrews 3:8-11 (NIV):

> *"... during the time of testing in the wilderness, where your ancestors tested and tried me ... I said, 'Their hearts are always going astray, and they have not known my ways.' So I declared an oath in my anger, 'They shall never enter my rest.'"*

MY PATH OF TESTING

My deepest testing came when God activated the second leg of my financial adversity — my Recession 2.0, beginning in 2014. Kim and I were just starting to feel better about our family's future after surviving the worst industry collapse since the Great Depression, to then suddenly lose 90% of my business all over again! But as I said previously, it was God's *silence* in that period of adversity that confused and distressed me the most.

You see, for the previous 10 years I had been diligently learning how to hear God's voice as a road map through life's twists and turns. I had a good bit of experience following God's words revealed both through scripture and through His *rhema* words. R*hema* words are intimate revelations God gives directly to an individual. These *rhema* words were vital for Kim and me to make it through our terrifying situation in the housing market collapse (more on that in Chapter 5). So, for God to suddenly be silent at this time was devastating to me.

As I said, this second financial wilderness was more difficult than the Great Recession. In the first year, God continued to bring miraculous provision as He had before (always at the last minute, I might add). But then things got worse by early 2016. So much so, that by the end of that year, I was forced to borrow money from my parents just to make ends meet. This was so difficult to do, not for pride reasons, but because Kim and I had seen God come through miraculously so many times before. We didn't deposit my parent's check right away, believing God would give us a miracle again. But this time no miracle came. We waited until the absolute last minute to deposit the check, before we would default on the big payments like the mortgage and medical insurance. Still no miracle.

This was crushing. I was numb with confusion and bewilderment. Why was God seeming to act so differently than He had up until now? It didn't make sense because our faith was truly in Him. Over the early months of 2017 things continued to get leaner and leaner for us financially, to the point we felt we were forced to put all options on the table. There were three big decisions we had to consider that would alleviate our financial desperation.

First, we asked God if we were to go get jobs — any jobs — just to pay the bills. To be clear, we had not been stubbornly resisting this idea up until now. We were fully willing to take any jobs we could get. Rather, God had given us clear direction not to do so back in 2009 (again, which I will reveal in detail in Chapter 5). The second option was to sell our home because, by now, it had a significant amount of equity that could help give us some financial breathing room. But if we did this, we would uproot our two kids from the wonderful school system and friend network they had known their entire lives. Finally, the third option was to borrow more money from my parents, who had come back to us with another gracious offer of a larger amount to help us stay afloat.

We prayed over these three options — a lot! We had many close friends and family members doing the same. We were fully surrendered and willing to accept any option, according to God's directions, though I stressed a bunch over them as well. However, though we sought God's leading with everything we had, He was still silent. So, we did not act on any of the three options. We both sincerely believed we were to stay the course in our wilderness regardless of how difficult it was.

Well, it turned out to be the right choice. Here's how: Kim and I simply did not sense that any of these options were right. To us, they were all an act of desperation which cut against the core of our truest and most honest convictions and desires (not our fleshly desires for comfort or materialistic happiness). Each option would have been a different "ejection button" out of our adversity, and they just didn't feel right to us. To put it differently, none of the three options seemed right in our "gut" — in our spirit — because in view of all that we'd experienced with God's miraculous acts thus far, we knew He had not brought us into this second wilderness just to leave us to figure things out on our own. We chose to believe He had not forgotten nor forsaken us, as He promised. We chose to believe in His goodness beyond our increasingly difficult circumstances. We chose to believe in God more than in any relief we could secure through our own efforts and options.

As I said, it was the right choice, because as soon as Kim and I were settled on staying the course, and we did not act on any of these three options, God showed up! And He showed up BIG! By the middle of 2017, God suddenly opened the floodgates of architectural provision. At this time, I was unexpectedly chosen to be the new lead designer for a high-end custom home builder I had just recently met. When we first met, I did not think anything would come of it because he had been working with a competitor designer. But two months after our meeting he called me out of the blue with five design projects ready to start immediately! One of them was to design the home of one of the highest paid NFL athletes of all time (I won't name-drop here because that's just tacky to do). To have a client of this level is something few architects ever achieve, but to have him handed to me with no effort of my own was a mind-blowing gift from God.

And He didn't stop there! I had two lucrative potential clients I'd been pursuing for over four years. I had already sent them design agreements on multiple occasions, but year after year, they always had reasons for not starting their projects. Then all of a sudden — and all at once — they were both ready to start! One of them was the largest design contract I've ever signed to this day.

But wait — there was more from God! Again, out of the blue, I was referred by a close friend to a builder who had just contracted with an investor from Atlanta to build custom homes for 39 lakefront lots in a very high-end waterfront community. Within two hours of shaking the builder's hand for the first time, I helped him close his first $3 million custom home client! Since then, we've formed an ongoing design relationship that has been one of the best I've ever had.

You see, God was testing Kim and me to see if we would trust our hearts' inclinations that God was not abandoning us to act out of desperation. We sensed *in our hearts* that the three options we were contemplating were not aligned with God's intentions for us. Our intense financial need did not overpower our belief that God still had a greater purpose for our adversity.

Don't get me wrong here, we were fully willing to do whatever was necessary in the midst of our financial wilderness. We were willing to take any job we could find, or sell our home to meet our financial obligations as responsible adults. But because of the many things God had taught and revealed to us, we believed He didn't require those options of us. God's words were vital to support this belief! And so, in the darkest hour of our adversity we did not act on any natural (and logical) sources of relief, thereby *unknowingly* passing His test with intense confusion and uncertainty.

Unfortunately, most of us fail God's tests of adversity because we do not know how to see the purpose of the wilderness He has led us into. Instead, we look for the quickest way out and miss the very *heart* of the matter. It turns out that exiting our adversity most often disqualifies us from God's Life-giving promise. That's the power of the next secret of the wilderness.

Adversity offers us the opportunity to see and repent of our natural commitments hidden in the unseen recesses of our hearts.

CHAPTER 4

SECRET #3: DISCOVERING A NEW WAY TO LIVE

"...to know what is in your heart..."

DEUTERONOMY 8:2 (NIV)

OUR HIDDEN CONFLICT

*T*he third reason God leads us into adversity is to allow us to discover what's in our hearts — *both the good and the bad.* The Apostle Paul reveals a fundamental conflict at the heart of our being:

"For the flesh desires what is contrary to the Spirit, and the Spirit what is contrary to the flesh. They are in conflict with each other, so that you are not to do whatever you want."

GALATIANS 5:17 (NIV)

Most people live completely oblivious of this war raging in their hearts — a war of desire. A conflict between the flesh, which relies on its own natural efforts to attain abundant Life, and the

Spirit, which is Life-giving and of God. Both seek Life to the full, but only one can provide it, and the other always results in spiritual death. Let's examine this conflict a little closer to find out why it's true.

We were all created with a real, God-given sense of desire within us — a fundamentally pure desire for abundant Life which God designed for us to possess without lack or fear of loss. In fact, all people intrinsically desire God because only God is Life — most just don't know it.

The problem is, we live with broken hearts in a broken world, both of which intensely compel us to secure our core desires for Life through sources apart from God. Our fleshly efforts and strategies are destined to result in disappointment. Our efforts to achieve what is unachievable outside of God require us to accept the counterfeits of better outcomes, pleasant circumstances, and positive results of our own making. We believe that we will finally be happy *"if only"* we worked harder or smarter, had the right job, the right girl or guy, the right amount of money, the nicer car, the nicer house, a certain education — the list is endless! But our efforts to attain true happiness through these outcomes under the sun will *always* leave us unsatisfied. Remember, nothing under the sun gives Life because nothing under the sun has Life to give.

Therefore, God leverages the inevitable adversities of life to save us from our chosen paths of futility. He uses pain and loss to give us the opportunity to see this conflict between our fleshly desires and the Spirit-given desire for Life. God's purpose in adversity is that we will come to our senses regarding the inefficacy of living for better outcomes and pleasant circumstances under the sun. Without loss and suffering, we will continue our insatiable quest to secure Life from natural things — which are mostly good things — but cannot give us the kind of Life God made us for. Adversity gives us the chance to see that our natural pursuits will never succeed. We must allow it to do its work in us.

THE COUNTERFEITS IN OUR HEARTS

Adversity quickly shows us how committed we are to living for ourselves — to saving ourselves through our own strengths and strategies. In fact, our self-sufficiency and self-reliance are the most significant obstacles to finding and walking God's path to abundant Life.

Though the Bible and its teachers have been very clear about our self-centeredness, we just can't see how deep it goes until we suffer hardship and loss. This is revealed through things like depression, anger, addictions, or affairs. These are the more obvious signs of our commitment to our broken expectations. However, it's crucial to realize that the vast majority of our self-preserving energies are considered normal and acceptable. It can look like an increased drive to secure some outcome we believe will turn things around (much like my marketing efforts to gain new clients during the recessions), or committing to spend more time doing leisurely or healthy things — even serving the homeless or our church. Yet even though our sources for happiness may seem benign, if they are based on natural outcomes and positive results under the sun, they will not satisfy our built-in need for Life as God intended.

So, whether it's having a stress-free life or a full-tilt one, we are all trying to find happiness and fulfillment through some outcome strategy of our own determination. Adversity offers us the opportunity to see and repent of our natural commitments hidden in the unseen recesses of our heart. Our fixation on better outcomes seems completely reasonable to us, yet they are lifeless counterfeits that reject God and His heavenly intentions for us. We must come to the end of our natural-mindedness in order to receive God's life-giving reality.

This is also true for those committed to full-time ministry. No one is exempt from this under-the-sun curse just because they "work for God." Whether someone is a wildly successful pastor or the compassionate founder of an orphanage in Calcutta, their godly work here under the sun will never provide the true contentment they seek. Life only comes through the person of Jesus Christ — not in our good works. No work or calling — no matter how godly — can give Life because none have Life to give. Therefore, adversity comes even to those whose work is committed to God, in order to reveal this unexpected reality.

No work or calling — no matter how godly — can give Life because none have Life to give.

A TRANSFORMATION CLOSE TO HOME

I grew up as a missionary kid in the Dominican Republic until I was 16 years old. My parents spent 20 years doing the "ultimate work" for God in four foreign countries. They were good people with good intentions (and still are), serving God the best they know how.

However, something seismic happened for them in 1988. We had moved back to the US as a family so my parents could get trained in biblical counseling. Their intention was to return and help heal the epidemic of broken families and marriages in the Dominican Republic. But God "ambushed" my parents with a healing of their own.

Through a series God-ordained circumstances, my parents were admitted to the Institute of Biblical Counseling, led by doctors Larry Crabb and Dan Allender. Now, don't let the academic title of that program fool you! This was an intense Christian "boot camp of the heart" my parents had unwittingly stumbled into. By the first six months, they had discovered more about their inner reality than they had ever imagined. One evening they sat my brother, sister, and me down in our rented home in Winona Lake, Indiana (yeah, that's where God took us from the Caribbean — sheesh!). My parents began to share some deeply hidden motivations which they had never revealed to us before. They also shared how they were discovering a whole new way of *living from their hearts*, rather than from religious duty and moralism. It was a life-reset of everything they had previously taught us.

In brief, my parents revealed how they discovered a subconscious deal-making arrangement they had made many years ago with God

We must discover and live from our new and good heart, or we will remain sadly discontent all the days of our lives.

to become missionaries. Their part of the deal was that they would sign up for the most "hardcore" Christian thing they could do. God's part of the deal was to heal their broken hearts that had been wounded by painful childhood experiences. In this counseling program, they discovered that after all those years they had become missionaries in order to get God to make them happy. Like I said, this deal with God was entirely subconscious to them. But once they discovered how their life choices were mostly byproducts of trying to find inner peace, validation, and healing, they were confronted with the reality of their hidden motivations behind their choice to enter such extreme ministry, like becoming missionaries.

Please don't misunderstand what I'm saying here. All of us are making choices every day of our lives, mostly out of a subconscious drive to find happiness, peace, security, love and meaning through better outcomes, pleasant circumstances, and positive results. This is completely normal to us. But this drive is fueled by the pain of our past no matter how good a childhood any person has had. Although few people are aware of what fundamentally drives them, we are all constantly motivated to find fulfillment for the lack we have in our hearts and lives.

My parents had their share of difficulties and pain in their childhood, creating a thirst in their hearts that needed fulfillment. Once they became saved, they were driven to work serving the Lord, which they did with genuine care and devotion, but also with a hidden motivation in the core of their hearts. Thanks to the life-changing work of Larry Crabb and Dan Allender (to whom I am forever grateful), my parents began the journey of discovering that God needed *nothing from them at all* to heal their past and satisfy their souls. He was ready to do that at any moment, with no obligations in return, except sincere surrender.

Since then, I've witnessed so many people in full-time ministry who are performing their profession well, but with mixed motivations. I truly believe they want to help others find salvation in Jesus and live godly lives. But I can also tell they are hoping for an extra measure of abundant Life as an outcome of "working for God." It's natural to think this way. I was falling for this lie as well. Therefore, God must use adversity as one of the most powerful means of helping us see the hidden motivations of our heart — if we are willing.

Adversity comes to us all. And when it comes to those who have given everything to serve God, it hurts more. If that's your story, adversity is meant to reveal how your deepest motivations originate from the same drive to find Life under the sun as everyone else. Just because your job serves others (and God) doesn't mean it has Life to give. Serving others will not give you Life because nothing under the sun has Life to give. Only Jesus is Life. Serving Him should come from a heart filled by only the real and abiding presence of Jesus — nothing more.

This is so important that I want to say it again: adversity offers the opportunity to see this deal-making mechanism hidden in all of us, which keeps us from gaining the very thing we desire the most. Again, our self-sufficiency and self-reliance are the most significant obstacles keeping us from finding and walking God's path to abundant Life. Until we truly and fully repent of our own efforts and strategies to secure Life for ourselves, we will never find it.

Therefore, we must acknowledge and engage this conflict in our hearts if we are ever going to gain the Life we so deeply desire. We must do the work required to win this war of our heart's desires — the flesh pitted against the Spirit. We must repent of the self-preservation that adversity exposes in our hearts.

DISCOVERING OUR LIFE-GIVING DESIRES

But remember, this is only *half* the story about our heart and its desires. Only when we are able to sift through our fleshly attempts at securing happiness — *and* we surrender them — can we begin to discover something new. We discover our true Life-giving desires, with which God originally created us to find fulfillment in Him, and Him alone. Adversity removes the layers of self-sufficiency in order to reveal *the good* that's in our heart.

There's one important requirement though: only those who are saved — who are born again — are able to discover the true desires God put in them. Salvation is required because it's the only way to receive a new heart, and only a new heart can receive abundant Life.

This reveals one extraordinary reality of being born again that is rarely discovered and enjoyed by most Christians: *we have a new heart which is good!* Only our new heart is able to connect to God's Life-giving presence. And only our new heart is capable of possessing the good and holy desires which God gladly and lavishly fulfills as we repent and surrender to His Life-giving reality. Therefore, God offers adversity to act like a spiritual defibrillator to awaken our new heart to come alive in Him, rather than through better outcomes or pleasant circumstances.

Living from our new heart is the only way to truly be content, even while we are in adversity. Otherwise, we are driven by the needs and desperation of our flesh to find satisfaction, which "profits nothing." Jesus revealed this shocking dichotomy in John 6:63 (NASB):

"It is the Spirit who gives life; the flesh profits nothing…"

Now, I must pause to offer a correction to a very misleading teaching about our hearts. Far too often, I've heard preachers and teachers condemn our hearts as a "lost cause" because of this one verse:

"The heart is deceitful above all things and beyond cure. Who can understand it?"

JEREMIAH 17:9 (NIV)

Here's the complete picture about this verse. First, it's absolutely true, but only about our natural fleshly heart. These words are being spoken directly by God Himself who is saying that our hearts are beyond cure — unfixable! That's why Jesus had to come down from heaven, die, and raise to life — so we could do the same. We must die spiritually in order to put our natural, incurable heart to death. But then comes the greatest news of all time: we too are raised to new life in Christ! We are born again as *a new creation* by the Spirit. Therefore, we have a new heart, which has good and godly desires!

Still not convinced that your desires can be redeemed from wickedness? Here's what the prophet Jeremiah says just five verses later (which I've NEVER heard taught in conjunction with verse 9):

"Heal me, Lord, and I will be healed; save me and I will be saved, for you are the one I praise."

JEREMIAH 17:14 (NIV)

Yes! That's what Jesus came to do! He came to heal us and save us from our *incurable hearts of flesh* in order to make us a new creation with a new heart, which can then receive the abundant Life He came to give us! What good would this offer be if we were left with deceitful and incurable hearts? None, of course! And so, many well-meaning Christians live in a prison of believing their hearts (and therefore, their desires) must be suppressed because they haven't been taught how to live from their new heart and godly desires. No wonder Christianity appears to have so little to offer our world today — one of the best things about it has been incorrectly blacklisted!

God offers adversity to act like a spiritual defibrillator to awaken our new heart to come alive in Him, rather than through better outcomes or pleasant circumstances.

THE BATTLE OF OUR CONFLICTED DESIRES

However, for the born-again Christian, receiving a new and good heart initiates a raging battle within us — a battle of opposing desires — as Paul revealed in Galatians 5:17. God is keenly aware of our conflicted situation, knowing that until we surrender to His healing intentions in adversity, we will never live from our new and good heart. Redeeming our hearts from its attachment to fleshly outcomes is one of God's main purposes in adversity. Paul continues to explain this conflict in the famous Romans 7 passage:

> *"For I know that nothing good dwells in me, that is, in my flesh; for the willing is present in me, but the doing of the good is not."*

ROMANS 7:18 (NASB)

> *"O unhappy and pitiable and wretched man that I am! Who will release and deliver me from [the shackles of] this body of death? O thank God! [He will!] through Jesus Christ (the Anointed One) our Lord! So then indeed I, of myself with the mind and heart, serve the Law of God, but with the flesh the law of sin."*

ROMANS 7:24-25 (AMPC)

Paul perfectly describes the battle of the redeemed heart versus the flesh. Our flesh desires the things which lead only to death — which is the result of putting our hopes in outcomes under the sun. Yet only through the work of Jesus are we set free from this bondage of the flesh. The problem is that most believers don't live from their new heart, missing out on freedom and Life. Rather, they continue to conform to the pattern of this world by seeking Life from the realm of the flesh which cannot give it. That's why

Paul proclaims that living according to the flesh is "unhappy and pitiable and wretched!"

And so, the importance of living from our new and good heart is to *discover our true desires*. This is critical because, as we've seen, living from our flesh generates desires that only result in discontentment, which is spiritual death.

> *"So letting your sinful nature control your mind leads to death. But letting the Spirit control your mind leads to life and peace."*

ROMANS 8:6 (NLT)

You see how discovering our true desires is of utmost importance? We *must* discover and live from our new and good heart, or we will remain sadly discontent all the days of our lives. We will remain prisoners to the curse of living for better outcomes and pleasant circumstances under the sun, even noble and well-meaning ones, which have no Life to give. And if we continue living according to our flesh, eventually our unmet thirst will lead us into dark places, resulting in despair or addiction — or both.

This is the lesson the Israelites never learned, and thereby forfeited their Promised Land. They never came to understand God's life-giving ways. Though they were chosen by God and experienced His miracles all those years in the wilderness, *the hunger of their flesh* drove them to crave natural gratification through better outcomes under the sun. This disqualified them from receiving God's life-giving intentions. And it still does today for all God's creation.

We don't have to live the way we've been living. We don't have to live like everyone else. We must discover this new way, which is to live from our deepest and truest desires by faith in the Life-giving reality of Jesus.

A NEW WAY TO LIVE

When we live from our new heart centered on Jesus (who is the Life-giving Spirit), we receive other-worldly joy, peace, love, and security (which is abundant Life). Living from our new heart frees us to desire the good things God has for us, rather than enslaving us to our flesh. Living from our new heart releases our desires from the bondage of striving to find fulfillment and satisfaction through our own efforts. Only then will our desires align with God's heavenly reality. And only then are we able to receive the abundant Life God has for of us.

So, in order to be abundantly clear about what abundant Life is, I want to offer this definition: it is *to gain our seven core desires of happiness, security, peace, love, meaning, validation, and relationships from the Life-giving presences of Jesus to the full, without lack or fear of loss, regardless of our circumstances.* These desires were designed by God to only be met *in Him*, not by anyone or anything else. Yet, because we were born and raised as worldly beings with fleshly desire, a Life-giving relationship with Jesus is far more unnatural to us than we can imagine. Therefore, God's purpose for leading us into the wilderness is to help us discover our true desires — those desires He put in us when He created us *in His image*.

Let me explain this from a personal standpoint. As a residential architect, I get great satisfaction designing dream homes for wealthy clients. From a worldly perspective, clients with greater wealth or fame can give me a sense of greater self-worth. They also equate to greater financial security, which I desire as well. In fact, I recently had the opportunity to bid on a job for a potential billionaire client. This was a first for me. And once I discovered I was on the "short list" of architects to be chosen for the project, I began to get really excited about what winning this level of business could provide for me in the way of professional validation, financial security, and overall peace and happiness.

But, in the end, I was not chosen. Yes, I was deeply disappointed. My mind quickly processed what I should have done differently: "Why didn't they pick me? Did I do something wrong? What must I do differently to win the job next time? *I can't let this happen again!*"

These thoughts revealed how my natural way of viewing this undesirable outcome involved an underlying sense of rejection, insecurity, and drivenness. My flesh raged with emotion to ensure better outcomes if another "high level" prospect like this came along my path again. This is the way of self-sufficiency. This is the path to bondage and lifelessness. I needed to repent for allowing my flesh to get the better of me in that process, and I did, in order to stop walking too far down that *other path* Jesus warned about — the one that leads to destruction.

What I did in this situation is completely natural to us because we all seek fulfillment in everything we do, whether consciously or not. Security? Yeah, we want that — we need it! Validation and meaning? Of course! But if we get below the surface layers of our feelings, we can begin to see that our true desires are for something else. We long for something more fundamental than winning a job, making more money, having more meaning or purpose in our lives — or whatever you're hoping for right now. We need abundant Life from the presence of Jesus because God made us that way. And guess what? Jesus claimed to offer that to us freely in Him, regardless of circumstances! That's why we must never seek our fulfillment in worldly outcomes — like staking my security and validation in landing a billionaire client.

Now, I feel I must clarify the term "worldly" in order to avoid some common misconceptions here. In the Bible, worldly desires don't only refer to sinful acts like abusing one's children, cheating on one's spouse, or lusting for wealth and power. Worldly desires encompass any desire for happiness, peace, and security through *natural human outcomes* here on earth, like having an enjoyable job, a loving spouse, or even a good church. Desiring worldly outcomes is completely normal to us. We were all raised to derive Life from worldly sources and results, no matter how godly the intentions of our parents, teachers, or mentors.

And since no outcome under the sun has the ability to give true Life, it's imperative to distinguish between our need for true Life and anything we do *in this life*. We must come to our senses to see that successes and accomplishments have no bearing on attaining true contentment, because abundant Life is not in them.

That's why Jesus came to offer us a different way to live in this world. A way that is centered on the Life-giving reality of His presence no matter what we do — no matter what happens to us. We don't have to live the way we've been living. We don't have to live like everyone else. We must discover this new way, which is to live from our deepest and truest desires by faith in the Life-giving reality of Jesus. Author John Eldridge explains that even Jesus had to live from His deepest desires in order to accomplish His purpose in this world:

> *"The 'joy set before him' enabled Jesus to endure the agony of the Cross (Hebrews. 12:2 NIV). In other words, his profound desire for something greater sustained him at the moment of his deepest trial."*

John Eldridge — *Desire*, 2010

In God's reality, we can be fully content even when we are in want!

Even Jesus had to endure His own wilderness of adversity in order to gain the Life He desired — which was to give Life to the world. Because of this reality, no matter how noble and godly your work and purpose may be, the work you do cannot give you true Life. True Life is found only in the person of Jesus Christ. Therefore, for those in ministry, be careful not to miss God's work in adversity even though you've been living as godly as you know how. He'll walk with you in it, and give you the desires of your heart *if* you learn how to surrender to His unnatural purposes in the wildernesses of life.

So many well-meaning Christians have spent a lifetime chasing after the "holy grail" of true Life through full-time ministry by becoming pastors or missionaries, only to find themselves empty and frustrated (at best), or painfully lost in severe depression and addiction (at worst). This disappointment and frustration of unmet expectations in life happens to all of us — to some degree or another — due to our fixation on fulfilling our desires apart from the Life-giving reality of Jesus Christ. There is a better way to live! There is a path that leads to abundant Life. And only adversity offers the most effective opportunity to find it.

Abundant Life is to be happy, secure, at peace, loved, and validated; living meaningful lives in healthy relationships to the full, without lack or fear of loss, regardless of our circumstances.

GOD'S UNSEEN REALITY

So then, if we are called by God to abandon our fleshly efforts to seek better outcomes and pleasant circumstances here in this world, then what are we to desire? What are we to seek? And how do we live happy lives apart from outcomes under the sun? The answer to these questions requires a new view of our desires *and* a new view of heaven:

> *Jesus came to Galilee, preaching the gospel of the kingdom of God, and saying, "The time is fulfilled, and the kingdom of God is at hand. Repent, and believe in the gospel."*

MARK 1:15 (NKJV)

Here, Jesus reveals a powerful, Life-changing reality that was not taught to me growing up in the Church. In fact, I've rarely heard this taught anywhere. There's a crucial paradigm-shift in this one verse that has been almost entirely missed for 2000 years! Jesus declared that the Gospel — the good news He came to earth to reveal — was to offer us God's kingdom which is within reach now. The kingdom of God (or the kingdom of heaven, as Jesus also called it) is God's realm where our truest desires are fully met *in Him*.

It's the place where water turns to wine, where seas are parted, and believers walk on water. It's where the mouths of hungry lions are shut. And it's where a young rejected boy defeats a warrior-giant with a single stone and becomes king of a nation. It's the world of the unseen and the unimaginable — where miracles are real and happen to those who earnestly ask for them! This is God's kingdom — *His heavenly reality* — that Jesus said is within reach now. This is the realm we are to desire. This is what we are to seek every day of our lives. Jesus was clear on this:

> *"Seek the Kingdom of God above all else, and live righteously, and he will give you everything you need."*

Matthew 6:33 (NLT)

In God's kingdom *He* is our happiness and peace, *He* is our security and love, *He* gives us our meaning and validation, regardless of outcomes and circumstances. This is the theme of the entire Bible! But we've missed this because we've been raised in the system of the world (through parents, schooling, the workplace, and even the Church) to get our happiness, peace, love, and security through natural outcomes and positive results.

We need to change our mindset to desire and constantly receive the heavenly reality God has for us *in this life*. It's much closer — and fulfilling — than people think. However, it can only be received by faith and not by sight. And, it can only be found by living from our true desires which flow from our new heart. Here's an example of what this looks like.

RECEIVING MY CAREER FROM GOD

When I began my college "career," architecture was not on my radar. In fact, I went to Georgia Tech to study electrical engineering. Though my first two quarters were a good start, by the third quarter I was failing — miserably. My final GPA that quarter ended up a 0.0. Yes, I failed *all* my courses, dropping my overall GPA to a 1.8! This was the first time in my life I had ever failed a class, and it wasn't for lack of studying. I was trying as hard as I could to pass my classes, but I had simply "hit the wall" where calculus II, chemistry, and computer programming were beyond my natural capabilities. I was now in a tough spot, having no idea what to do with my life as a young adult.

In order to figure out a carrier path at this juncture, three fairly improbable things needed to happen in the short term: 1) I needed to get a job to pay for my next quarter in school, which was the obligation my wise and understanding parents required of me for failing my previous quarter; 2) I would have to reapply to Georgia Tech, requiring their acceptance in light of my terrible standing; and 3) I would need to figure out what to study, since engineering was clearly not the path for me. So, I looked to God and asked, *"Lord, what do you have for me?"*

Well, over the course of that summer, all these needs were met in a way that was clearly God's doing (I mean, would you let me back into your college with a 1.8 GPA? Yeah, neither would I!). So, it was to my great surprise that Georgia Tech did accept me back (on academic probation, of course), and at the suggestion of a friend who knew me pretty well, I decided to give architecture a try.

God's words are always leading us to Life — true and gratifying Life.

Therefore, we must seek and nurture a conversational relationship with Him in order to find it.

I was immediately smitten! Architecture, it turned out, fit me like a glove, and I went on to graduate from Georgia Tech with a respectable GPA, and a wonderful career in hand. But I never would have come up with that extraordinary plan for my life on my own. Rather, God led me through my self-inflicted failure as I opened myself up to His realm — to His heavenly reality that was within my reach through faith and surrender. This resulted in revealing my truest desire for work, and a career that I still successfully practice to this day. This significant life experience at the beginning of my adult years showed me that God's unseen realm of blessings and provision cannot be found by my efforts or wisdom. It could only be received by surrendering myself to God and His heavenly reality that is always near to me. In fact, all the stories I share in this book came from this heavenly reality.

There's an important distinction I want to clarify here. In my academic story, I needed some important outcomes and circumstances to become a reality for me, like finding a career in which I could succeed. But, to be clear, I did not go to God with a list of my expectations in hand. I didn't tell God what to do, or what I expected from Him. Rather, I surrendered my need for better outcomes and pleasant circumstances to *His* wisdom and arrangement. I only asked God for the good He had for me in His kingdom — and that's what He gave me. And so, since He knew how he made me far better than I did, *He* arranged for outcomes that made me very happy.

As Christians, we may seek God's will. We may pray for Him to open and close doors as we try to make godly decisions (by the way, I don't believe God is a "doorman," but that's for another book, I guess). Most often when we pray, our underlying expectations toward God are almost always about *our* "wish list" of better outcomes and circumstances. It's mostly about getting God to make our life more pleasant and positive, and less painful and difficult. Instead, He wants to show us what He made us for, and the extraordinary gifts of Life and purpose He has in store for us, which are beyond our imagination (and our failures). We must ask God the simple prayer I prayed, rather than fixate on specific outcomes we think will make us happy. We must pray:

"Father, what do you have for me?"

Forgive me for being blunt, but I believe 99% of all Christian living (and prayer) is essentially trying to "rub the lamp" the right way to get the "God-genie" to show up and grant our natural wishes, which come from our fleshly desires. And because of this broken approach, God must resist our fleshly commitments, because if He grants us our requests, He will reinforce our wrong thinking by doing so. Instead, He must leverage the adversity and pain in our lives to challenge this false approach to life. God's goal is to lead us to find Him and Him alone as the only sufficiency of our true desires. Paul reveals this unnatural, other-worldly way to live in Philippians 4:12 (NIV):

"I have learned the secret of being content in any and every situation … whether living in plenty or in want."

Sure, we all get excited about being content with plenty, but did you catch the part where Paul says he discovered the secret to being content *even when in want?* This reveals the paradigm shift of God's kingdom. *In God's reality, we can be fully content even when we are in want!* Let that sink in. This is entirely unnatural to us! It's not normal. It's not human nature. In fact, isn't being *in want* how we define being *dis*content? But that's why God had to send His Spirit to dwell in us. It's the only way we can live from His kingdom reality. His kingdom contains the fulfillment of our desires that our heavenly Father wants to give us — and it's within our reach now!

I feel I must continue to repeat a common misconception that those who pursue full-time Christian ministry as their work tend to make. No act of our own, no matter how godly and noble, has the ability to give us Life — to truly satisfy and fulfill us. It certainly feels good to help others, but that outcome of goodness is just as fleeting as an illicit drug high. I'm not saying good works are ungodly. Not at all! I'm saying good works — even godly works — *don't have Life to give.* They never have. They never will. Isaiah made this abundantly clear:

> *"…all our righteous acts are like filthy rags; we all shrivel up like a leaf, and like the wind our sins sweep us away."*

ISAIAH 64:6 (NIV)

Our most righteous acts cannot give us Life because they have no Life in them. *Only Jesus does.* If we seek to satisfy our desires for happiness, peace, security, and validation through godly acts of service or ministry, we will eventually become disillusioned and discontent. Jesus calls us to find true and lasting fulfillment in Him and Him alone. We will only gain true Life to the extent we live from our new heart and discover our true desires — desires *He* satisfies through His ever-present kingdom of abundant Life.

THE LONG JOURNEY TO MY TRUE DESIRES

So far in my life, I've experienced four unique episodes of intense adversity — the first one beginning when I was 30 years old. Three of them were work-related adversities and one was the loss of a deeply meaningful and enjoyable ministry I co-led with some great men. All my difficult experiences were created by ordinary economic and human influences which had negative and painful impacts on me. Yet God was always ready and willing to leverage these hardships for my transformation to a greater understanding of His unseen reality (like how God led me to my career, though I had failed miserably through my own strength). While each of my adversities was unique, one aspect was consistent in them all: God wanted me to live from my new heart and true desires. Here's what that looked like for me:

As I've mentioned, my career has been designing multi-million-dollar custom homes for wealthy people. This particular work has been held in very high regard for, well, thousands of year. It's considered an elite profession, and given an extra measure of respect in society. The problem is that this kind of job can offer good income and a lot of validation. So, my flesh naturally wants to maximize that outcome by any means possible. It's easy to get caught up in working hard to increase success to shore up as much financial security and validation as possible. Success on these two fronts, I thought, would then give me more peace and happiness. We all naturally do that.

So, when the housing market collapsed in 2008, top economists were predicting that the outlook for my profession, by all historical and economic measures, would be a wasteland for at least the following 10 years. This decimated my ability to gain any kind of security and validation through my work. This "elite" career became a *"vapor and a breath"* in a very tangible way!

God's greatest goal in all the adversity I've experienced has been to help me discover a deeper reality of my desires for success. He led me into multiple wilderness experiences and *"caused me to hunger"* financially and emotionally, in order to help me discover two critical realities: first, I needed to see the futility of my self-reliant efforts and strategies to secure true and lasting happiness; and second, I needed to see that only Jesus is the true fulfillment of my core desires for happiness, peace, security, and validation.

The same thing happened when that wonderful ministry I deeply enjoyed was taken away. I won't go into details, but it was entirely unexpected. This sudden loss added a deeper degree of discouragement and confusion to my adversity because it was a good and godly work. People's lives were being changed through it — including my own. I loved the people and the outcome this amazing ministry was serving.

The loss of both this wonderful ministry and my business success were fundamentally necessary because God wanted to show me the hidden reality of my desires. Through the absence of income, success, and ministry, the Holy Spirit wanted to show me how I had misplaced my desires and expectations on Lifeless things. This did not become evident to me until my fourth wilderness — my "Recession 2.0."

While each adversity had its own redemptive purpose, all were intended to lead me to a singularly important understanding: that *I would never be truly happy until I found my contentment in God alone, regardless of any success — or lack — I may experience.*

This became clear 17 years after my first wilderness experience, and my view of securing happiness through outcomes achieved

God's words lead us through the wilderness journey we would never naturally choose to follow, so that we can receive the abundant Life we will never possess through our own efforts.

under the sun finally came to its insidious and stubborn end. The result has been a completely new view of my desire for happiness, which I will describe in detail in Chapter 6.

But remember, we're on a journey to find the path to abundant Life Jesus promised. God's ultimate intention is to bring us to a true Promised Land, a land flowing with the desires of our good heart, which can only be found in Him. The next purpose for which God leads us into the wilderness reveals God's "secret weapon" for guiding us to our promised land of abundant Life.

CHAPTER 5

SECRET #4: GOD'S LIFE-GIVING WORDS

"He did it to teach you that people do not live by bread alone, rather, we live by every word that comes from the mouth of the Lord."

DEUTERONOMY 8:3 (NIV)

WHAT ARE YOU "FEEDING ON?"

Without bread (food), we die. But God knows we have a greater need than just nourishment for our bodies. He knows that without His words — which is food for our souls — we will never truly live. To be clear, the passage above is not referring to literal bread. Bread in this passage represents all the outcomes we hope will satisfy our emotional hunger in this life. Bread also refers to all the broken addictions and sins we bring into our life in an attempt to anesthetize our pain and disappointment. This passage is calling us to get honest about the worldly bread we "feed on" in an attempt to satisfy our longings.

The Israelites in the wilderness literally lacked food, but God wanted them to look beyond their physical needs and deal with the hunger in their hearts. Similarly, we may lack a spouse, money, health, or a fulfilling job or purpose. In this passage, God is saying:

> *"Don't live by having a good marriage, enough money, a healthy body, or a fulfilling career. Rather, live abundantly by my Life-giving words, even if you remain single, in poverty, physically limited, or jobless."*

I know, I know, this does NOT sound like abundant Life! But this reveals the humanly inconceivable divide between the natural and the spiritual realities God is presenting us in Deuteronomy 8:3. God is revealing the nourishing reality of His words to satisfy our hunger exposed in adversity. His words always lead us to Life — true and gratifying Life. Therefore, we must seek and nurture a *conversational relationship* with God in order to find it. Only God's words offer true and lasting contentment and satisfaction, even when we are in want.

Unfortunately, most people, including Christians, do not have a conversational relationship with God. In fact, most people barely have any relationship with God at all. And even for those who are committed Christians, the kind of relationship which *"lives by every word that comes from the mouth of the Lord,"* is far deeper than a "quiet time" relationship with Him. It's a relationship that is ongoing throughout the day, every day. But this kind of relationship doesn't form out of diligence or discipline. Only those who discover how utterly dependent they are on God for the fullness of Life they desire will receive it through fierce and unnatural surrender. Only God's words can reveal His abundant Life! We must live by His every word leading us along the path that few find — or we'll never find it either.

But there is another level of "bread" revealed throughout scripture that we must discover as well. It's the bread that *all* of scripture is revealing. We must discover the divine and satisfying *Bread of Life!* Here's the greatest offer of all times from Jesus Himself:

> *"For the bread of God is the bread that comes down from heaven and gives life to the world." Then Jesus declared, "I am the bread of life. Whoever comes to me will never go hungry, and whoever believes in me will never be thirsty."*

JOHN 6:33 & 35 (TNIV)

Jesus is speaking about the hunger and thirst of our souls here — *the true desires of our heart!* And He's saying *He* is the only true satisfaction of them — *He* is the fulfillment of our desires. It's important to understand the life-and-death reality of His offer here. Jesus made this clear a few verses later in John 6 when He said, *"Your ancestors ate the manna and still died."* You see, He isn't referring to their physical death here. The entire passage is about spiritual matters, and manna was a God-given thing just like a calling, gifts and talents, or a ministry. This means we can give our entire life to doing the work God called us to do, and yet still *never have true Life,* if we expect to get Life from the godly work we do. This is why so many people burn out after years of sacrifice and service. So many have given everything to a ministry or a godly purpose expecting inner contentment, only to end up with starving hearts and famished souls.

That's why adversity is meant to *amplify* our discontent — our hunger. Yes, you read that correctly! We must become increasingly more discontent with our natural strategies for satisfaction and fulfillment, in order to *feel* the hunger we've been masking our entire lives. God's purpose in hardship and pain is to bring us face-to-face with the subtle, ever-present hunger in our hearts we've become so good at anesthetizing. He does this in order to awaken us to the insufficiency of living from the "bread" of this world.

This Deuteronomy passage says it starkly, though it's easy to miss by reading right through it: *"man does **not** live on bread alone."* Re-read this a few more times. Can you hear the totality of our condition here in this world? God is revealing that there's *nothing* we can "feed on" under the sun that will give us Life because nothing under the sun has Life to give. Even God-given callings cannot give Life because *only Jesus is Life*.

Adversity is meant to amplify our discontent — that subtle, ever-present hunger in our hearts we've become so good at anesthetizing — in order to awaken us to the insufficiency of living from the "bread" of this world.

OUR SECRET BLISS

Here's one way to discover the life we believe would make us feel satisfied and happy. It's an exercise that can reveal those better outcomes that are the "bread" we long for in our lives. This involves something I believe we all do. Picture yourself driving along a highway and you see that large lottery billboard with the Powerball and Mega Millions prize money. Imagine winning that kind of money! And what do we all do then? We daydream about our life changing in an instant — a new life free from financial worries, full of happiness and blissful satisfaction. After all, we now have enough money to make all our dreams come true, right? That dream life — should we attain it somehow — is our "bread." It's the outcomes we believe will finally satisfy the hunger and thirst in our hearts.

Yeah, I'll admit I used to go down that fairytale path every time I saw those lottery billboards — until I realized what I was doing. I would daydream of a life where everything was the way I longed for it to be: living on a white-sand beach, in a home I designed, where I don't have to work unless I want to, and I can travel with my wife and kids anywhere, anytime (oh yeah, and give generously to those in need, of course).

It may seem like harmless daydreaming, but I believe it reveals something crucial in our hearts. It reveals that we have abundant life scenarios we long for, which we believe would become a satisfying reality through lots of money. What's your scenario? Or, to use the language of Deuteronomy 8:3, what "bread" do you believe will make you happy? If it's anything other than the Life-giving presence of Jesus, it won't truly satisfy, because nothing under the sun has the power to quench the thirst and satisfy the hunger of your soul. And so, adversity gives us the opportunity to discover the Lifelessness of "bread" under the sun.

JESUS' LIFE-GIVING WORDS

So, what's the antidote to "bread" that does not give Life? It's found in God's call to live by His words — both His "logos" words (which are the written scriptures) and His "rhema" words (which are the intimate words God speaks to us individually). We must discover that God's words give far more than instructions and directions — *they give Life!* Jesus revealed this power of His words, though it's easy to miss:

> *"...the words that I have spoken to you are spirit and are life."*

> **JOHN 6:63** (NASB)

Rather than dreaming of winning the big jackpot — or any other desirable outcome under the sun to provide us with abundant Life — we must instead include Jesus' words in our daily happiness equation. Yet, this is completely unnatural for us to do, but it's a supernatural reality we must experience in order to receive the abundant Life God has for us. He will lead and fill us using both His logos and rhema words as we live in a conversational relationship with Him.

> *"If you abide in Me, and My words abide in you, ask whatever you wish, and it will be done for you."*

> **JOHN 15:7** (NIV)

Do you see how lavish God's offer is here? *"Ask whatever you wish ..."* This kind of offer has been the thing of myth and fantasy, yet Jesus made this promise 2,000 years ago! Imagine how many wishes we've all missed out on because we've been abiding in outcomes under the sun rather than abiding in Jesus. We *must* learn God's scriptures and hear His voice, otherwise we have nothing better than to continue chasing the world's Lifeless counterfeits. Here's another Life-giving promise in the midst of scarcity and pain:

> *"Don't worry about anything; instead, pray about everything. Tell God what you need and thank him for all he has done. Then you will experience God's peace,* **which exceeds anything we can understand.** *His peace will guard your hearts and minds as you live in Christ Jesus."*

PHILIPPIANS 4:5-6 (NLT)

The only way to make it through God's wilderness journeys is to feed upon His words because His ways *"exceed anything we can understand."* In our natural viewpoint and rationale, we will shrink back from God's wilderness path. Therefore, we must depend on the guidance He offers through scripture and the intimate words He speaks to His children. His words lead us through the wilderness we would never naturally choose to follow, so that we can receive the abundant Life we will never possess through our own efforts.

Only in adversity can we begin to discover this supernatural gift hidden beyond our natural reality. Only by surrendering ourselves to God as He leads us through our wilderness experiences, can we receive the Life-giving power of God's words. This is the only way. Jesus has revealed our absolute need to surrender to His life-giving reality:

> *"For whoever wants to save their life will lose it, but whoever loses their life for Me (to gain Me) will find it. What good will it be for you to gain the whole world, yet forfeit your soul?"*

MATTHEW 16:25-26 (NIV)

To me, this is one of the hardest teachings in the entire Bible. Who lives their life to lose it? The answer is simple: *no one!* However, as the inevitable disappointments and adversity of life come to us, God offers us a *hidden path* to gain the very thing we seek. It's hidden because it's illogical to our natural way of thinking. I believe only the wilderness of adversity has the opportunity to reveal this hidden path to us, but only *if* we are willing to surrender our preconceived ways of finding Life. The Bible repeatedly reveals that God is offering us something beyond our comprehension. This is expressed quite clearly in 1 Corinthians 2:9 (NLT), which is one of my favorite verses in the Bible. Paul said:

> *"No eye has seen, no ear has heard, and no mind has imagined what God has prepared for those who love him."*

I believe the only way to receive God's unimaginable good is to submit to God's Life-giving purposes in the wilderness of adversity. And I believe the only way to discover and appreciate such inconceivable things from God is to have our human outcomes and expectations *removed from us.* Yes, this is hard to accept! But otherwise, we will continue to cling to whatever is natural and familiar to us, despite its inability to give us the abundant Life God created us for. In fact, our natural attachments keep us from finding it, no matter how noble they may be! This is why living in a conversational relationship with God is so vital — His words reveal the path to Life *which our mind cannot conceive nor imagine.*

GOD'S WORDS REVEAL HIS REALITY

It's imperative that every person understand and believe that God's words reveal how everything works — how we work, how

To find the Life we desire most, we must learn to believe in God more than we believe in our circumstances.

We must learn to see what is unseen as more valuable and more important — even more real — than what is seen.

relationships work, how Life works. God's words reveal His intended reality to give us what our eyes have never seen, what our ears have never heard, and what our minds cannot naturally comprehend. This hidden reality is revealed to us all throughout God's scriptures. Here are a few examples:

Walking on water

Peter and the disciples found themselves pushing agains a strong headwind at night on the Sea of Galilea — which means they were going nowhere fast while exerting a lot of effort doing so — which sounds like life sometimes, doesn't it? Jesus comes to them walking on water — certainly something no eye had ever seen. Astonishingly, Peter wants to give it a try, but he's keenly aware he has no authority to do such a thing. So, he asks Jesus to call him out to Him upon the water. Jesus says, "Come." Peter then steps out of the boat, *connects with God's heavenly reality,* and walks on water! But as soon as Peter shifts the focus of his faith off of Jesus and onto the howling winds and waves around him, he immediately reverts back to the laws of nature, and sinks.

Now you may be asking, "Mark, how in the world could this possibly apply to us today?" Well, as I've already shared, when God brought me miraculous architecture work in the midst of the "storm" of the housing market collapse to save my family and me from bankruptcy, He caused us to walk on water *financially.* God can apply the miraculous act of walking on water to any storm — a marriage storm, a health storm, a business storm, a church split storm. But there is one very important condition to this unnatural experience: we must hear God's voice before we start jumping out of whatever uncomfortable, scary, or painful situation we are experiencing. Like Peter, we must *hear Jesus calling us out* of our place of darkness, otherwise we will move in presumption and self-reliance. This is the great danger of "lighting our own torches" I referenced in Chapter 3 which God revealed in Isaiah 50:10-11.

All-you-can-eat miracle bread

One time, during the early years of starting my architecture firm, God used a story I could barely remember in order to save us. You see, at this particular time Kim and I found ourselves running dangerously low on income (you know, start-up business issues). She was home full-time raising our daughter, making me the sole breadwinner. Seeing our desperate financial situation, she turned to me one evening and asked, "What are we going to do?" I replied uneasily, "I don't know." But in my heart, I prayed my favorite prayer to God: *"Father, what do you have for us?"* At that very moment, the faint remembrance of a particular Bible story came to my mind, but I could only recall an instance in the Old Testament where oil and flour miraculously didn't run out.

It's the story in 1 Kings 17:1-24 (which I highly recommend you read), where a widow is cooking her last meal for her son before they starve to death due to a severe famine (which God brought upon her country, by the way). Yet because of her faith in giving her final meal to the prophet Elijah instead of keeping it for her son, *she enters God's supernatural realm* where the last portion of oil and flower don't run out for three years, until the famine ends!

You see, because I had read this story at one time (many years back), the Holy Spirit was able to bring it to my mind when I asked God what He had for us in our time of need. The Bible is full of these kinds of stories where God comes to the aid of people in need with His supernatural power and miracles. They're not meant to make the Bible appear mystical and out of reach to us. They're meant to reveal that a *supernatural* reality is available to us today in the midst of our *natural* existence. These stories teach us how to engage this miracle reality, especially if we find ourselves in need of one.

As our situation connected with this ancient story, which I believed was brought to my remembrance at that very moment for a reason, Kim and I chose to surrender to its lessons of faith in the midst of our similar need. We both believed that God was showing us that He would lead us to His supernatural provision *if* we were willing to receive it from His heavenly realm. This meant that our hearts and minds had to resist desperation and self-sufficiency. We focused our hearts and emotions on God's goodness expressed in this particular story, rather than dwell on our dangerous financial situation.

And so, within two weeks God brought a client to me who ironically was in an unusual hurry to have me design his home. You see, he was a disaster reconstructor — a builder who specializes in rebuilding businesses that have had a flood or fire. His specialization is speed, which requires that all his tradesmen are on his payroll in order to ensure they are not pulled away to other jobs like independent subcontractors. At this particular time, he had no contracts, and so all his tradesmen were idle even though he was still paying them their full salaries. So, he wanted them to build his new home before a new contract would require them to be consumed with a reconstruction project. I was able to get a fair fee *plus* a "rush order fee" on top of it, which he was happy to pay — and quickly! It was the perfect amount and timing we needed to avoid any financial defaults on our end. God's word revealed His *unimaginable path* to the good He had for us. All we had to do was receive it from His heavenly storehouse by faith in

Him rather than giving up on my business and finding a job elsewhere.

All biblical stories reveal that the only way to find the abundant Life Jesus said He came to give us is to know what God has to say on the matter — to experience the power of His Life-giving words. This is far different from our natural inclinations. To know God's words about true Life is to know scripture, where He reveals His intentions about Life from the first page to the last. Those who do not know God's words *will suffer great loss* by missing out on His endless abundance that is ready to be unleashed from His heavenly realm *right this second*. Here's how powerful Jesus reveals this unseen reality to be:

> *"I tell you the truth, if you had faith even as small as a mustard seed, you could say to this mountain, 'Move from here to there,' and it would move. Nothing would be impossible."*

MATTHEW 17:20 (NLT)

LIFE-GIVING FAITH

God's goal is to grow us up to live by faith and not by sight because He knows something about faith we consistently miss: *faith is believing and staking our lives in God's unseen reality above our human reality.* Therefore, to find the Life we desire most, we must learn to believe in God *more* than we believe in our circumstances. We must learn to view what is unseen as more valuable and more important — *even more real* — than what is seen.

"The godless world can't take [the Spirit of Truth] in because it doesn't have eyes to see him — doesn't know what to look for."

JOHN 14:17 (The Message)

This is why the Bible — God's word that reveals the path to Life — is full of outrageous stories like killing giants, walking on water, unending flour and oil, and raising the dead. These are the examples God has intentionally given us to learn from and apply to our own journey. He wants us to live as if impossible outcomes are possible in our daily lives. This can only happen as we live by faith according to God's words here under the sun.

Yet God knows that the most common disqualification to living by faith is living by sight — not sin. Sin is what comes next when we live by sight. When we live our lives hoping and banking on human outcomes here under the sun, we will entirely miss God's Life-giving kingdom, which is within reach at all times. Instead, we must believe in and take hold of God's unseen reality by faith.

"...[God] is able to do immeasurably more than all we ask or imagine, according to His power that is at work within us..."

EPHESIANS 3:20 (NIV)

And so, in adversity, God gives us the opportunity to turn away from the natural outcomes and strategies we believe will make us happy. If we are willing to take Him up on His wilderness mission, He will transform us into people who can receive true Life from His unseen kingdom. There is simply no other way to it.

God's discipline in adversity is designed to teach and form us into the kind of people who can find and walk the path to Life that Jesus said few find.

God wants us to live as if impossible outcomes are possible in our daily lives.

GOD'S WORDS SAVED US!

My family and I would have been financially destroyed by the Great Recession had it not been for God's words. He spoke through His scriptures and He spoke through His Spirit, to lead us in ways Kim and I never imagined. Here's how it happened:

The housing market collapse was sudden, fast, and frighteningly deep. What made matters worse for all of us in the industry was that we simply didn't know how bad it would be. So, we all made the same devastating mistake: we kept spending the money we had trying to find new work. It was a futile effort, which only accelerated our financial demise.

And so, as the economic news continued to worsen, so did my level of fear and distress. One night, I was up late in bed unable to sleep due to intense anxiety. I was watching every news channel in order to be as fully aware of the economic situation as possible (which certainly didn't improve my emotional state). Finally, one chief economist on a news show said these dreaded words:

"The housing market is in a depression, and will likely be so for a long time — most likely 10 years or so."

These words were like a punch to the gut. My head dropped into my hands in disbelief that my once prosperous and wonderful profession had become my worst nightmare. Images of the Great Depression flashed through my mind of men standing in soup lines because they had nothing else with which to support their families. I turned off the television and collapsed back in bed, my heart racing with fear as I was confronted with such a devastating reality that I was completely unable to avoid or overcome. I then did the only thing I knew to do. Out of desperation, I asked God one simple question:

"God, we don't have the ability to survive this! What do you have for us?"

That's all I could muster. I stayed quiet, my eyes shut, but my heart and mind were searching, listening for God. Then a thought came to me, as if it had been spoken into my mind by someone else:

"Go read about David."

I knew these weren't my thoughts because my mind was consumed with panic and fear — not an ancient Shepard boy. Rather, it was God speaking into my thoughts.

For a second, I was perplexed. Why did God feel I needed to read about David? God was fully aware I knew David's story inside and out — after all, he was my favorite character in the Bible. Yet without hesitation, I reached into my nightstand and pulled out my Bible, the one given to me by my father when I was 12 years old. I've loved this book and have studied it diligently ever since. And so, I knew where to find the story of David, introduced in the middle of the first book of Samuel. But that night, God showed me something I had never seen before — something I desperately needed!

As I re-read the familiar story, I came to the point where Samuel was about to anoint David's oldest brother as king, but God interrupted him.

> *"When [David's brothers] arrived, Samuel saw Eliab and thought, 'Surely the LORD's anointed stands here before the LORD.' But the LORD said to Samuel, 'Do not consider his appearance or his height, for I have rejected him.* **The LORD does not look at the things man looks at."**
>
> **I SAMUEL 16:6-7** (NIV)

That last sentence jumped out at me, like the volume in my mind had been turned up as I read it. I had never seen it before. It gripped me.

Then God spoke very clearly to me. He said:

> *"I'm not looking at the news you're watching."*

I was convicted and humbled, but I responded:

> *"I know Lord, but … are You seeing what's happening? It's really bad!"*

God gently replied:

> *"I don't have this for you."*

These words startled me. I quickly asked the Lord for clarity:

> *"What do you mean? What don't you have for me — this recession?"*

At that moment I could sense the conversation was over — like a phone call when you know the line has gone dead. There was no answer to my question, no clarity for this cryptic message. So, with a desperation to see if the rest of David's story could help me understand God's words, I dug back into the Bible. In fact, I spent the next *four years* reading every story I could find in the Old Testament. Because of my adversity, I now had "new eyes" for the wild hair-raising stories in the pages before me. I could now put myself in their shoes and feel their desperation, fear, and confusion. But I also saw God's amazing and unexpected acts, which one-by-one, broadened my expectations of God showing up for me in this economic nightmare.

Nonetheless, by early 2009, I could see the end of our finances coming fast. I was considering every angle for work, even serving coffee at my local Starbucks to allow me the flexibility of doing design work, if it came in. I reached out to a close friend, Hanna, who had worked there for a while to get the inside scoop. But then, God raised the stakes to a frightening new level.

I was now in the habit of asking God "the question" every day — usually 20 times a day: *"Father, what do you have for us?"*

This time He gave me a direct answer when I asked specifically about pursuing a position with Starbucks. He clearly said:

"Stay the course."

I needed no clarity with what God meant. I understood that I was not to seek any employment whatsoever and remain solely focused on residential design work — in spite of the lack thereof. This was a difficult word to process because God did not provide any certainty regarding the outcome of doing so. He didn't give me a

God's discipline often requires the removal of things we believe are necessary in our lives in order to show us His unexpected and unnatural path to true Life.

revelation of how to make ends meet. He gave no assurance we wouldn't lose our home. So, I asked God for confirmation that this was indeed His words, because the stakes of getting this one wrong were extremely high.

In an abundance of grace and mercy God immediately provided two amazing confirmations. The next day, I nervously told Kim what I had heard from God. I was fully expecting her to find this idea as hard to accept as I did. Yet to my shock, she replied how she had heard the same thing! This was an extraordinary relief to me since now I didn't have to convince my wife of the outrageous idea of following me over the financial cliff based on *my* conversations with God. So, we both intensified our prayer to confirm that God was truly calling us to go *all in* with this risky directive. The next day Hanna called us, insisting that both of us be on the phone to hear something she and her husband Bob wanted to tell us. They too, had been praying for us, fully knowing our situation, but completely oblivious of God's recent instructions to us. She said they both clearly sensed God wanted us to "stay the course" with my design work rather than get a second job elsewhere! Kim and I were astounded! We were so thankful and relieved that God would be this considerate of our natural insecurity regarding this dangerous word from Him. These confirmations made God's word undeniable to us.

And so, we did just that. We stayed the course. But our bank account did not. It continued to dwindle down to our last $700 by the early days of the summer of 2009. This was the first time we didn't have the mortgage payment (among many others). And while it came with an eerie feeling, Kim and I were not terrified. We were 100 percent committed to the path we believed God called us to walk. We had no assurances of outcome. We had no

The pain of adversity is a necessary "antidote" to help us give up on our naturally held beliefs and convictions — which do not give Life.

assumptions that God would come through and save our home and financial situation. We simply knew what God had said, and we followed His direction.

Then … God showed up! My phone suddenly started ringing off the hook with new clients! I proceeded to receive more business in the following six months than I'd ever secured in such a time period — and none of it was from seed I had sown. It was truly a miracle. God had saved us by His words! Had we ignored God's frightening instructions and followed the logical course of action by taking any job to pay the bills, I'm certain we would have eventually lost our home to foreclosure. So many other people in the housing industry (who were much wealthier than I was, by a long shot) were losing everything. Instead, God's words were the *hidden path* through this certain failure. But they required complete and utter belief in Him rather than in our circumstances.

As you know, however, this was not the end of our adversity. There was more wilderness for Kim and me. There will be for all of us in this life under the sun. So, we must press on into the unknown, living by every word that comes from the mouth of the Lord. For He desires to bring us into a new kind of relationship with Him. The next purpose of our wilderness journey is designed to bring us closer to God than we've ever imagined.

CHAPTER 6

SECRET #5: GOD'S LIFE-GIVING RELATIONSHIP

"Just as a parent disciplines a child, the Lord your God disciplines you for your own good."

DEUTERONOMY 8:5 (NLT)

GOD'S LIFE-GIVING DISCIPLINE

*A*ny parent understands how naive children are to the dangers in the world around them. Good parents teach their kids to look both ways before crossing the street, to eat right, and play nice with others. The goal of any good parent is to raise children who will not harm themselves or others by living undisciplined and senseless lives. Discipline teaches children how to live good and safe lives. And when understood and accepted, discipline also provides rewards and freedom in life.

Likewise, we all require spiritual discipline. But this is a much deeper work than we naturally understand. God's desire is to raise children who will not hurt themselves or others through natural living — that is, by living for outcomes under the sun. His goal is the same as any good parent: raise children who live abundant lives for eternity. And because God is keenly aware of the eternally destructive reality of natural living, He sent Jesus to give us this crucial warning:

> "...wide is the gate and broad is the road that leads to destruction, and many enter through it. But small is the gate and narrow the road that leads to life, and only a few find it."

MATTHEW 7:13-14 (NIV)

God wants what's best for us. His discipline in adversity is designed to teach and form us into the kind of people who can find and walk the path to Life that Jesus said few find. It's not meant to punish us. God knows we punish ourselves enough already through natural living! His discipline is strategically designed to give us the opportunity to find the path to Life, and live it with everything we've got.

But there's one massive difference between well-meaning human parents and God: God will allow His children to experience a lot of pain, sometimes even horrifying tragedy, to wean us from our addiction to natural human living. God is willing to allow — and even inflict — adversity on His children. Yes, this idea is disturbing! It may even sound heretical to you, but there is plenty of evidence throughout the Bible of God being directly responsible for all kinds of calamity. Remember this unnerving verse I mentioned previously?

"I am the LORD, and there is no other; I form the light and create darkness, I make peace and create calamity; I, the LORD, do all these things."

ISAIAH 45:6-7 (NKJV)

Throughout the tumultuous relationship God had with the Israelites, He repeatedly warned them that if they didn't put their full trust and faith in Him, He would bring famine or enslavement against them. And He did, many times. Even though the 10 plagues inflicted upon Egypt were not directed against the Israelites, they so enraged Pharaoh that he made the Israelites' lives miserable — to the point they begged God to stop doing anything that would irritate their slave master. But God didn't stop. Instead, He turned up the intensity with each new plague, and Pharaoh increasingly penalized the Israelites in turn.

The ultimate act of God inflicting intense adversity is found in our salvation. The horrific conclusion for Jesus to come to earth was for Him to suffer and die an excruciatingly painful death. This was part of the plan from the beginning, and when Jesus asked His loving Father for a different way, He said, "No."

But remember, Jesus was able to endure the pain of His mission on earth because His hope was fixed on the *"joy set before Him,"* which was the liberation of God's creation by taking back all authority in heaven and on earth. That reward was worth it to Jesus. Likewise, we must believe God is good at all times and that His plans will always result in great reward for those who trust Him. So, when He brings adversity into our lives, it's because He knows natural human living (living in the flesh) is infinitely and eternally harmful. In fact, God calls it *death*. As a good and loving Father, His discipline is wholly focused on getting us to see the tragically ineffective reality of our natural ways. In addition, He knows how great the reward is that He yearns to give us — the reward of His abundant Life.

Consider the following two versus which reveal the totality of the situation our heavenly Father is intent on saving us from:

"…you have no life in yourselves."

JOHN 6:53 (NASB)

"… a man's way is not in himself, nor is it in a man who walks to direct his steps."

JEREMIAH 10:23 (NASB)

These verses reveal what we're up against. I challenge you to consider the colossal implications of these two short verses. The very thing we desire and need the most — true and abundant Life — has not been in us our entire lives! No wonder the thirst of our hearts is never met. And no wonder we keep defaulting to the natural ways of finding satisfaction which never work — which God says lead to death!

"For the mind set on the flesh is death, but the mind set on the Spirit is life and peace…"

ROMANS 8:6 (NASB)

If we don't come to grips with this reality, that we and the world around us lack the very thing we need the most, then we will languish in increasing discontent all the days of our lives. This is why Paul warns us:

"…do not conform to the pattern of this world, but be transformed by the renewing of your mind."

ROMANS 12:2 (NASB)

God's word has been warning us all along to avoid the lifestyles which result in inner death and destruction, which are the outcomes of living according to the world and our flesh. Unfortunately, most people are tragically unaware that many common activities they practice in their lives qualify as *the patterns of this world* that do not lead to Life. This broad instruction covers far more than just blatant sinful living. It also includes all the good, wholesome, and noble living through which we seek better outcomes and pleasant circumstances here under the sun.

And so, God uses adversity to expose our natural tendencies to getting our needs met through lifestyles which conform to the patterns of this world — again, lifestyles which most often aren't even directly sinful. God's discipline often requires the removal of things we believe are necessary in our lives in order to show us His unexpected and unnatural path to true Life. This is illustrated by God removing the Israelites from Egypt where, though they were slaves, they had all their needs met. Yet as free men and women in the wilderness, the frightening scarcity quickly caused the Israelites to long for the security they previously had *as slaves*. God's intention for bringing them into the wilderness and causing them to hunger was to give them the opportunity to believe in God to meet their truest needs as a good and loving Father, rather than depend on the security offered by their slave masters. We must allow God's discipline to do the same in our lives. We must believe that He is leading out of slavery to this world and its lifeless outcomes, and into a promised land of abundant Life.

Against all logic and reason, the wilderness of adversity is the required path to receive God's greatest good.

Every promised land requires a wilderness — or two, or three.

THE FOOLISHNESS OF GOD'S WAYS

God's discipline is a very difficult thing to believe and accept. I've reminded God many times that we humans have laws here on earth against some of the things He is willing to inflict on His children. I'm not being irreverent here. It's true. God is so committed to arranging circumstances that will give us the opportunity to let go of our natural worldly commitments, that He will allow — *and even cause* — tragic events in our lives. Like I said, we have laws against that kind of parenting here on earth (and rightly so). But God is not subject to our laws because He is up to something far beyond what we can imagine. Therefore, He will use unique means of getting us there — methods and circumstances we will often consider unkind or even unloving in our natural human system. God has been abundantly clear on this:

> *"For my thoughts are not your thoughts, neither are your ways my ways," declares the Lord. "As the heavens are higher than the earth, so are my ways higher than your ways and my thoughts than your thoughts."*

ISAIAH 55:8-9 (NIV)

The good Life God desires for us is far beyond our natural understanding. Most often, the path He requires to possess His abundant Life will be foolishness to our natural senses and beliefs. Paul revealed this frightening reality we all struggle with.

> *"But a natural (worldly minded) man does not accept the things of God, for they are foolishness to him…"*

1 CORINTHIANS 2:14 (NASB)

God's "foolish" ways are our Heavenly Father's acts of "tough love." And if we'll surrender to Him in our adversity, He'll transform us into sons and daughters who can receive the abundant Life He has for us. God never intended for our world to be this way, yet it is. And so, in order to fully honor our free will, He will lead us into adversity designed simply to give us the opportunity *to choose His ways over our ways.* The pain of adversity is a necessary "antidote" to help us give up on our naturally held beliefs and convictions — which do not give Life.

This is one of the fundamental secrets to the story of Job. As I previously mentioned, Job is declared righteous by God Himself at the beginning and the end of this horrifying story. However, Job's limited understanding of God's ways and values caused him and his three friends to stumble around looking for a reason he deserved such suffering. Instead, God had the ultimate Life-giving encounter of His presence in store for Job. It just required severe desolation as a prerequisite. This one verse was the entire point of Job's suffering:

> *"I have heard of You by the hearing of the ear; but now my eye sees You …"*

Job 42:5 (NASB)

It's a harsh and unnatural reality when circumstances lead us into painful adversity no matter how righteously we've attempted to live. However, without the wilderness, God knows we will cling to the world's system — which is death to us, and unacceptable to our heavenly Father. God will discipline us in order to give us the opportunity to see His Life-giving reality, if we are willing. It's not punishment, though it may feel like it. Again, the natural results of fleshly living is punishment enough. God's goal is to lead His children to a better way to live — *like any good parent does for their children.*

God knows that true and lasting happiness, peace, love, and security are at stake. He understands how natural it is for us to seek these human needs from things here under the sun. He also knows that our natural preferences and strategies all result in spiritual death. So out of His infinite love for us, His sons and daughters, He will use the circumstances that have the greatest chance of leading us back to Him and His Life-giving reality. This will almost always look and feel like foolishness. We must see it as His path to Life *for us.* We must choose to follow Him through the wilderness, rather than *fight our way out of it* through our own wisdom and abilities.

If you're in adversity right now, I encourage you to stop everything you're doing right now and surrender yourself to God's ways. He loves you more than you could ever imagine. But He also knows the massive danger you are in if you continue to seek fulfillment and satisfaction from natural means. Trust Him today to know what He's doing, even if it looks and feels like foolishness to do so.

> *"There is a way which seems right to a man, but its end is the way of death."*

PROVERBS 14:12 (NASB)

131

God has a lavishly abundant promised land for us in this life. But His ways of getting us there — always through the wilderness of adversity — are foolishness to us.

Therefore, we must believe in His goodness more than we believe in our difficult circumstances.

The good Life God desires for us is far beyond our natural understanding. Most often, the path He requires to possess His abundant Life is foolishness to our natural senses and convictions.

AT MY WITS' END!

Remember Psalm 107:23-27 from Chapter 1? I want to revisit this verse again because it is very real to me in my story:

> *"Some went out on the sea in ships; they were merchants on the mighty waters. They saw the works of the LORD, His wonderful deeds in the deep. **For He spoke and stirred up a tempest** that lifted high the waves. They mounted up to the heavens and went down to the depths; in their peril their courage melted away. They reeled and staggered like drunkards; they were at their wits' end..."*

At my wit's end — that's exactly how I felt during my next round of God-induced adversity — my four-year "Recession 2.0." I knew God had stirred up this next tempest in my life because it wasn't happening to anyone else, and there were no tangible reasons for it to occur. There were also two additional painful aspects to this particular wilderness: first, this second round of financial adversity was more intense than the housing market crash; and second, God was surprisingly silent when I needed His clarity and direction the most.

The courage I had gained through our miraculous experiences of God's rescues during the housing market depression slowly melted away as the months of this unexpected wilderness turned into years. Again, no matter how hard I tried, my efforts didn't result in any relief. I clearly sensed God was blocking my every move to fix our frightening financial situation.

If this idea of God making things harder and more painful for me is disturbing to you, I get it! It doesn't seem right for a good God to stir up storms in our lives, to then hinder us in our efforts to find solutions and relief. But this is one of the most important and life-changing breakthroughs I discovered in all my adversity. I discovered that God so deeply desires abundant Life for me, that He is willing to use any means necessary to give me the *opportunity* to find it. He never violated my free will. I had complete volition to tap out and improve my circumstances through natural outcomes anytime I wanted. But Kim and I both had enough spiritual awareness to know we would be rejecting God and His unfathomable ways if we did so, there by rejecting His heavenly plans for us.

So, we continued to believe the direct words He spoke to us five years before: *"Stay the course."* But to be clear, even though we chose to live by faith, we were both at our wits' end. I was intensely anxious about making ends meet. Neither of us knew what would happen next. How deep would God take us? Would we lose our home? Would we lose everything? We knew from the "great cloud of witnesses" in Christian history that much greater hardship had happened to much greater believers. From their stories, we knew things could get worse — much worse. But we continued to believe God was up to something we couldn't yet see and understand.

I discovered that God so deeply desires abundant Life for me, that He is willing to use any means necessary to give me the opportunity to find it.

In the midst of all this, I kept digging into the Bible and realized God did the same thing to every single person who attempted to follow Him! Though this offered no relief (I'm sure it doesn't to you either), it encouraged our resolve to persevere, seeing the same pattern of God's word playing out in our story. This connection to the patriarchs of faith helped us to simply hold on to our gut belief that God would eventually do something great, because that's what He did to every single person in the Bible who followed Him. Kim and I chose to believe in God's ways revealed in His scriptures more than we believed in our terrifying circumstances. God's rhema words revealed that this was all part of God's plans for us as well. Plus, we weren't going to be like *that one guy* who, when the Israelites saw they were trapped against the Red Sea with Pharaoh's army speeding toward them, said:

> *"Why did you bring us out here to die in the wilderness? Weren't there enough graves for us in Egypt? What have you done to us? Why did you*

This is the ultimate good
God has for us:

Jesus is the Life we desire,
even when He doesn't fix
our broken or painful
circumstances.

make us leave Egypt? Didn't we tell you this would happen while we were still in Egypt? We said, 'Leave us alone! Let us be slaves to the Egyptians. It's better to be a slave in Egypt than a corpse in the wilderness!'"

EXODUS 14:11-12 (NLT)

So, Kim and I "held on for dear life." We held on to our belief that God was fundamentally good and ultimately had good for us. We simply chose to believe in Him more than in our circumstances. We chose to believe that He's a good father who knows what He's doing.

If we are to receive the good God has for us, we must submit ourselves to His discipline *as His children*. We must trust He knows far more than we do. Even when our circumstances feel like God has abandoned us, we must believe He has a greater good in store for us — *as a good Father*. Discovering God's inconceivably great good is the next step in our wilderness journey. If we're willing to press on, what lays ahead will make our suffering fully worth it!

In light of all the stories of those in God's Word, the secret to receiving God's great good is hidden in a place most people never comprehend.

The ultimate good God has for us is hidden in the truest desires of our heart.

CHAPTER 7

SECRET #6: GOD'S UNEXPECTED SOURCE OF LIFE

"...to do good for you..."

DEUTERONOMY 8:16 (NASB)

GOD'S DEEPEST DESIRE

*F*inally, we've gotten to the "good stuff!" Yes, God wants to do good to us. His deepest desire is to bless His creation! This can be found all throughout the Bible, as God consistently blessed those who were committed to Him — *and He blessed them lavishly!*

He wants to bless *you* lavishly as well. He really does!

He created us out of His abundant goodness, and even though we've rejected Him, His goodness is still fully available to us today. God's willingness to give His Son over to death on our behalf is the ultimate proof that He is fully committed to doing good to us. And because of Jesus, sin is not the obstacle we believe it is (or that we might have been taught or told by others). Jesus tried to make God's desire to bless His children abundantly clear when He walked among us:

> *"So, if you sinful people know how to give good gifts to your children, how much more will your heavenly Father give good gifts to those who ask Him."*

MATTHEW 7:11 (NLT)

Our heavenly Father wants to give us all the good He has for us. It's His core desire. It always has been. But something stands in our way. Something keeps us from believing *and receiving* this heavenly offer. Our biggest obstacle is our flesh — our natural-mindedness. You see, since birth, we've been taught to be self-sufficient and self-reliant. We've been raised to be on our best behavior, get good grades, go to a good college (to get more good grades), get a good job, make good money, have a good family, and so on. All of this is supposed to add up to a life of happiness, peace, security, love, and meaning. Our flesh lives this way by default. We live this godless way automatically every second of every day. Even our most righteous moments do not release God's blessings upon us. *Only belief and surrender in His goodness does.* I feel it's important to revisit Isaiah 64:6 again because it reveals the inadequacy of our view of ourselves:

> *"...all our righteous acts are like filthy rags; we all shrivel up like a leaf, and like the wind our sins sweep us away."*

We have to get this! We must realize that nothing in this world, no matter how good and noble it may be, can give us the Life we were created for — the Life we fundamentally desire. Therefore,

God's ultimate desire
is that we would see
Jesus as the abundant
Life we so desperately
desire.

we must shed the incorrect views we've been taught over the course of our lives if we are to find true Life. We must abandon our self-reliant quest to find Life apart from God in better outcomes here under the sun. But this is completely unnatural to us.

And so, against all human logic and reason, the wilderness of adversity is the required path to receive God's greatest good. Every promised land requires a wilderness — or two, or three. This is not because God is a drill sergeant whose goal is to train us into tough spiritual soldiers. The purpose of the wilderness is to remove the obstacles that keep us from receiving the great good God has for us. He gives us the opportunity hidden in adversity to give up on our natural default-mode of seeking better outcomes and pleasant circumstances in this world. If we are willing to do so, His desire is to truly satisfy the thirst we were born with *through His presence*.

The purpose of the wilderness is to remove the obstacles that keep us from receiving the great good God has for us.

If we do a quick survey of biblical stories, the vast majority of them end in great good and victory. Again, remember Psalm 107:23-27 about merchants on the waters who were at their wits' end in terror and dismay? The passage concludes quite nicely, in fact:

> *"Then they cried out to the LORD in their trouble, and he brought them out of their distress. He stilled the storm to a whisper; the waves of the sea were hushed. They were glad when it grew calm, and* **he guided them to their desired haven."**

We all have an idea of what will make us happy, a "desired haven" we're seeking with everything we've got. No matter if that haven is a simple life or a fast-paced one, God will frustrate our natural strategies to give us the opportunity to choose a different way, to find and follow a *hidden path* to the great good He has for us. He promised this to His people as He led them into their wilderness:

> *"For the Lord your God is bringing you into a good land... a land where bread will not be scarce and you will lack nothing..."*

DEUTERONOMY 8:7-9 (NIV)

Isn't that what we all want — to lack nothing? To have all our needs met and all our desires satisfied? The promised land God had in store for the Israelites didn't just meet their needs, it was an over-the-top wonderland that was lavishly abundant! This is where God is leading you, if you will surrender in faith to His ways. God has a lavishly abundant promised land for you *in this life.* But His ways of getting us there are foolishness to us because our flesh will always require the wilderness of adversity ... or two, or three. Therefore, we must believe in God's goodness more than we believe in our difficult circumstances.

Only when our heart is drained of our self-sufficient efforts to find Life through outcomes under the sun can we truly seek God with all our hearts.

Only when we've given up on the natural results the world offers to secure happiness will we discover God's lavish joy to bless us supernaturally.

GOD'S UNEXPECTED SOURCE OF LIFE

Once we begin to discover that God's path through the wilderness is a journey toward receiving the great good He has in store for us, we must discover something new about God's *ways* — something unexpected. The way in which God bestows His good upon us is different from what you might have been taught as a Christian. Let me explain.

First, there's a myth out there I want to clear up. So often, I've heard well-meaning Christians say, *"God's desires must become our desires."* It's not true, to the extent I hear most people speak of it. Most often, this idea means that our desires have to be entirely replaced by God's desires. This may sound right, but I believe our true desires — our seven core needs — to be happy, secure, at peace, loved, validated, and living meaningful lives in healthy relationships *are* God's desires for us. Those are the desires God put in us when He created us in His image. The difference between godly desires and fleshly desires is always *the sources we seek* to satisfy our core desires. I don't believe we must replace our core desires. Instead, we are to replace our sources of gratification and fulfillment from outcomes under the sun to God's life-giving presence.

For example, we all have a desire to be gratified sexually. We were created this way. Yet, how we gratify this God-given desire is what becomes a matter of right or wrong. God wants us to be sexually gratified because He made us that way, but He wants us to do so in accordance with His original design and intent. To go against His intentions for sexual gratification will result in death — morally, relationally, personally, and sometimes even physically.

Now, if a married person has a desire for someone other than their spouse, this is not a core desire. Rather, their God-given core desire is for love and relationship. If they are not experiencing that with their spouse, God's word explicitly forbids seeking any fulfillment for intimate love and relationship outside of the marriage. The "desire" this person has for someone outside of God's marriage design is not a core desire, but rather it's a demand to have their core desire met by fleshly means.

The same goes for *all* of our core desires. We do not need to change our core desires, we need to change how we seek to fulfill them. This is the ultimate obstacle between us and God's Life-giving promise. Since God's ways are not our ways, He is calling us to live very differently than we naturally do. Therefore, to become godlier people does not require different core desires, it requires a transformation to seek the fulfillment of our true desires in a different way — in Jesus alone. He is the fulfillment of our true desires, regardless of our circumstances and outcomes.

Let's look at how this applies to money. God made us to have total and complete security without fearing lack or loss. This is a core desire He put in us. Again, it's how He made us. But in our broken world, this kind of security is impossible to find, even if we have unlimited amounts of money. If we work in such a way that our faith is in our job and paycheck, we have misplaced the fulfillment of our core desire for security in an outcome under the sun. The core desire for security does not need to change, but rather the source in which we seek its satisfaction. Notice the consequence of the love of money in this verse:

"For the love of money is the root of all kinds of evil. And some people, craving money, have wandered from the true faith and pierced themselves with many sorrows."

1 Timothy 6:10 (NLT)

This doesn't mean we don't work or pay our bills, expecting money to fall out of heaven. That's not how God works, even though He could do it. It means we follow God's ways to receive our security from His heavenly storehouse. This also means we must have a deep understanding of God's words, both His logos and rhema words, in order to know what He has to say on the matter. We must discover His hidden path — His kingdom reality which is at hand — regarding our desire for security. In contrast to the verse above, notice the opposite effect of godliness over greed, according to God's word:

"But godliness actually is a means of great gain when accompanied by contentment."

1 Timothy 6:6 (NASB)

This is true of every other category in our lives. Therefore, we must deeply analyze our expectations in life in order to differentiate our core desires from the *objects of our desires*. The difference is seeking God for Life versus seeking outcomes. Here's an amazing example of this divine paradigm shift.

A COURAGEOUS STORY OF DESIRE

My friend, Margaret, had been single for 60 years, serving the Lord as a missionary. Since decade after decade she never found a husband, she began to believe that perhaps God wanted her to remain single. But one day, during a life group gathering in my home, I asked Margaret to share what she dreamed about — what were the desires of her heart. With tears in her eyes she admitted she longed to experience the love of a husband. I shared with her how I believed that meant God intended for her to be married. This was hard for her to receive because she had accepted the single life as God's will in order for her to be more available to her ministry work. I invited her to believe that her desire for marriage was built into her *by God*. But Margaret pushed back. *"If that was the case,"* she asked, *"then why have I been single my whole life?"*

At our next gathering, I shared that I believed a key culprit might be found somewhere in her story. So I asked her to share her life story with the group to see what we could find. Sure enough, she revealed a life-changing experience for why she had spent so many years alone. Margaret revealed how she grew up with an older brother who bullied her incessantly. One particular day when she was eight years old, during another barrage of cruelty, her brother snapped at her saying, *"You're never going to get married!"* It stung her deeply. At that innocent and vulnerable age, she wondered if there was something wrong with her that made her undesirable. And because her young heart was untrained to defend itself against such attacks, she bought into her brother's lie and believed it throughout her life. Of course, once becoming an adult, she found a more acceptable framework to rationalize the possibility of perpetual singleness by believing God had called her to serve Him alone. Plus, now sitting in this life group decades away from those seemingly unimportant childhood experiences, she was at an age that confirmed marriage was not in the cards for her. *"It's what God has for me as a missionary,"* she said, with a tinge of forced assurance.

I immediately responded, *"Margaret, there's something there — in that statement from your brother. I believe that message initiated a childhood belief — a false one — that has contributed to why you've been single all these years. It's not what God has for you if you have the desire to be married. If God really gave you the 'gift of celibacy,' then you would be fully content being single."*

I suggested she renounce that lie, which she had unwittingly accepted from that wounding experience so many years ago. She agreed, and I led her in prayer to receive the restorative healing Jesus offers to all who ask. Margaret also did something brave that evening. She acknowledged and proclaimed her desire to be married — before a group of married thirty-year-olds — even though it seemed like wishful thinking.

Now, God often requires our belief to "marinate" in unmet desires for a period of time. He does this to test us, to see if we will conform our will to believe in God more than our undesirable circumstances — to see if we will give up on our old worn out attempts to make life work without Him. This waiting period is a crucial stage to God's work in our adversity. Here's an amazing glimpse of how Margaret immersed herself in God's presence — and how she ultimately received the desire of her heart.

During that prayer time, I offered Margaret a scripture passage from Hosea as encouragement that God wanted to speak to her about her willingness to open up her heart to her desire for a husband. In Hosea 2:14 (NIV), God says:

"Therefore, I am now going to allure her; I will lead her into the wilderness and speak tenderly to her."

After that meeting, Margaret dug into this passage and found something stunning in verse 16 that I had not seen myself:

"In that day," declares the Lord, "you will call me 'my husband;' you will no longer call me 'my master.'"

HOSEA 2:16 (NIV)

This passage gripped Margaret's heart and she realized God was speaking directly to her through it — He was wooing her to Himself as the true fulfillment of her desires! She believed that God was calling her to see Him as her true husband. And so for the following months, she took long walks to focus her heart on God being her husband, meaning, she intentionally opened her heart to receive *God's presence* as the spiritual fulfillment of her desire for a husband. She shared with me how she prayed on her walks. She would pray:

"Lord, I've accepted You as my Savior, as my Lord, as my Father, and Jesus as my friend. But now, I fully embrace my desire for a husband, and I invite You to fulfill this desire for me in new and wonderful ways. And, Heavenly Husband, if you desire to give me an earthly husband, then you know that I'll need him to be the best that only You could provide."

Well, God loves an opportunity to show off — and He did! Within one year, Margaret was married to a wonderful man who loves ministering as much as she does! God gave her the desires of her heart because it's His desire to do so! But the biggest obstacle that hinders God from doing good to us is our lack of belief in God's heavenly reality more than our natural reality. Margaret had to receive healing from her past, reconnect with her true desires, hear and receive God's words for her, and then align her beliefs with His heart toward her.

GOD'S CIRCUMSTANTIAL BLESSINGS

Just like with Margaret, many stories in the Bible show us how God most often blessed His faithful ones with *the very thing they desired!* Here are a few well-known examples:

David is a rejected son and a lowly shepherd boy with no future, yet he has the intense passion and skill of a godly warrior. We see this in how he cares for the sheep in his charge, risking his life to kill attacking lions and bears. God also confirms this with the epic win over Goliath. Yet David is forced into a 10-to-15-year-long wilderness exile before he becomes God's promised king. David had no chance whatsoever to become anyone of significance in his own wisdom and strength. Yet through David's long and enduring belief and obedience, God gave him the greatest manifestation of the desires of his heart — God made David king of Israel with an undefeated record in battle as well.

Abraham was part of a Bedouin family, whose only safety was in numbers. Since Bedouins didn't build cities, they didn't have protective walls. Therefore, they could only survive by sticking together and growing as large a community as possible. Anyone who attempted to live alone faced certain pillaging and death. But what does God say to Abraham? He tells him to take his family (his wife, children, and servants), leave his clan (the extended family which offered protection), and go where God tells him. The

God is ready to release miracles in the midst of adversity to show us how to walk with Him in it, rather than expect or demand that He remove us from it.

He seeks a relationship of belief in Him, rather than belief in His power alone.

problem is, God didn't tell him where to go. Abraham was expected to just go anywhere away from the protection of his family and clan!

What's amazing is that, despite the lack of a specific destination, plus the certainty of extreme danger, Abraham takes God at His word and leaves his clan! But now he faces a life-threatening problem: Abraham has suddenly become an easy target for deadly mercenaries who were widespread in those days. If found, Abraham would immediately be killed, and his family and possessions would be taken as slaves. God expected Abraham to believe in Him more than the life-and-death dangers of leaving the protection of his family.

Now, here's the amazing promise God gave Abraham for believing and obeying Him: God promised to make Abraham's family the largest family of all time. It's so important to understand the power of this promise. This is *exactly* the desire of any person in Abraham's time and situation. Of all the things God could have promised Abraham, this was top of *his* list. Since Abraham believed in God's supernatural safety more than his earthly needs (as real as they were), God then fulfilled his natural desire, after all.

Joseph is given two divine dreams of greatness, yet he had to endure 14 to 15 years of the *exact opposite* before extraordinary prominence is bestowed upon him. His adversity was orchestrated by God to save the lives of many people, including his own family. Only after Joseph remains obedient in the face of severe and agonizing servitude does God fulfill the dreams of greatness He gave Joseph in the beginning.

Job's story is one of the most well-known stories of adversity. Though he suffers unthinkable loss, his great wealth and family are doubled as a secondary reward to the greater gift of seeing God with his own eyes as revealed in Job 42:5. As I mentioned in Chapter 3, God blesses Job lavishly:

> *"So the Lord blessed Job in the second half of his life even more than in the beginning."*

JOB 42:12 (NLT)

Jesus is the greatest example of God rewarding adversity. As I mentioned in the previous chapter, Hebrews tells us that a great reward was offered Jesus to accept the intense adversity of the cross:

> *"For the joy set before him he endured the cross, scorning its shame, and sat down at the right hand of the throne of God."*

HEBREWS 12:2 (TNIV)

To me, this sounds like a great reward being offered a warrior for accepting a dangerous battle — a worthy and desirable prize for undertaking a treacherous mission. So, what was this great reward being offered Jesus to endure such pain?

> *"Then Jesus came to them and said, 'All authority in heaven and on earth has been given to me.'"*

MATTHEW 28:18 (TNIV)

Wow! Do you see what happened there? God the Father rewarded Jesus with complete authority over heaven and earth. This wasn't just a participation trophy or a heavenly "attaboy." This promise of authority was Jesus' *truest desire* because it was necessary for Him to take back the authority Adam and Eve had lost back in the Garden of Eden to the serpent (the devil). Once Jesus took this authority back by enduring the cross, He then had the authority to revoke the devil's stronghold upon mankind, and was then free to be the Life-giving Spirit we needed Him to be in order to gain the abundant Life we were made to live. This has always been God's desire for us. This was Jesus' truest desire as well. Therefore, He accepted the adversity required to gain the authority necessary to restore *our* true desires — which is to have abundant Life *in Him!*

In light of all the stories in God's Word, the secret to receiving God's great good is hidden in a place most people never comprehend. The ultimate good God has for us is hidden in *the truest desires of our heart.* This is what good parents wish for their children — that they discover their *own* desires for their *own* lives. Our heavenly Father does the same thing. He longs for us to discover our true desires hidden in our new heart which Jesus made available to us through His suffering and pain.

That's why, in the wilderness of adversity, God's goal as our Father is that we discern what's in *our* hearts — both the good and the bad. First, God attempts to root out those fleshly desires which drive us to settle for futile outcomes here under the sun. And as we begin to understand our fleshly mechanisms, we must repent of them, or they will continue to rob us of the fulfillment of our true desires. God longs for us to realize that our fleshly desires are *not* our true desires. Then, through the hunger we endure in adversity, He invites us to discover the deeper, truer desires in our heart that only He can satisfy.

I must revisit an important distinction. I'm talking about something far deeper and much more Life-giving than finding "your calling" in life. Living out your calling is a great thing, but it cannot give Life — even if it's in ministry. No matter how noble, helpful, and self-sacrificing our God-given calling may be, it doesn't have Life to give. Sure, we feel good when we've helped someone. But so does an atheist!

That's not the Life I'm talking about. That's not the Life Jesus said He came to give us. True Life, abundant Life, is found *only in the person of Jesus* apart from anything we experience, possess, or do. He said it clearly:

> *"I am the way, the truth, and the life ..."*

JOHN 14:6 (TNIV)

To me, this verse is the single most powerful statement any human being has ever uttered! In these nine simple words, Jesus claims *He is everything every person is seeking*. Everyone is looking for their path to life, a truth to believe, and a life that is happy and fulfilling. Jesus claimed He is all those things. *He is what we're after!*

But Jesus' proclamation in this verse as the Life we are seeking is so far beyond what we first understand it to be. Many years ago, I realized that I had unknowingly distorted these words — I had reinterpreted them to fit my paradigms. It's something I think we all do. I subconsciously changed Jesus' words to say:

> *"I will show you the way, teach you the truth, and give you life."*

See what I did? I made it transactional. I subconsciously rearranged this wonderful promise about Jesus into something I can gain by my own achievements, like earning a PhD or a promotion. But it doesn't work that way. The true Life God has for us — the Life He made us for — is not an outcome, or a religion, or way of life; *it's a person*. Abundant Life *is Jesus*, and only Jesus. Furthermore, Jesus cannot be gained or achieved. He is only **received**. Abundant Life is not an outcome He gives. It is Him. He *is* the Way we're desperately trying to find. He *is* the Truth we're searching so hard to know. He *is* the Life we're dying to possess.

But I have to be very honest with you here. I must admit that it was incredibly disappointing to me when I realized that Jesus is the Life I seek. Sure, I wanted Jesus. But I didn't have an understanding of Him *as Life itself* apart from better outcomes and pleasant circumstances. You see, I wanted Him to *help* me get abundant Life. I wanted Jesus to team up with me to make my life more pleasant — make it better. I wanted Jesus to leverage His limitless power and resources on my behalf the way I would if I had them at my disposal.

But He rarely works this way. To our dismay He allows — even causes — adversity to assault our expectations. And then, instead of offering us His limitless power and resources, *He offers Himself* as our solution.

His greatest desire is to offer His presence because *His presence is Life-giving!* Most often He does this without leveraging His power to fix our broken circumstances or change our undesirable situations. He must operate this way because He knows something we don't. He knows that better outcomes and pleasant circumstances do not give Life. They certainly feel better than bad ones, but beyond how we feel, pleasant circumstances do not lead to the fulfillment of our true desires according to how God made us. I know I'm sounding a bit like a broken record with this, but God's desire in adversity is *to give us the opportunity* to give

It's not about money. God doesn't need money to give you a prosperous life.

He is Life. He gives Himself, which fills us with happiness, peace, love and purpose. God wants to give us Life to the full, abundant Life, because He made us for it.

That's why it hurts so bad not to have it!

up belief in better outcomes and pleasant circumstances here under the sun. And in so doing, God's ultimate desire is that we would come to see Jesus as the abundant Life we so desperately desire. If we don't get this, we will remain empty and discontent the rest of our lives, no matter how comfortable and successful we may become — or worse, addicted to sinful lifestyles.

So, how does this work? How is Jesus Life to us? Well, to answer that ultimate question, we first need a new view of Jesus — a far greater view than we've ever had.

A NEW VIEW OF JESUS

It starts by seeing Jesus far differently than we see Him now. We have to see Him as the Life we've thirsted and hungered for our entire lives. We must be transformed to see the person of Jesus as the fulfillment of our true desires. When we begin to see Him correctly, He then gives us Life by giving us Himself — His presence. Life comes to us when He shows up and His presence fills our hearts and minds, because that's who He is. In 1 Corinthians 15:45 (AMPC) Paul reveals:

> "The first man, Adam, became a living being — but the last Adam (Christ) became a life-giving Spirit ..."

The best example I can give of this Life-giving reality of Jesus' presence is similar to a drug trip (yeah, stay with me on this one). When a person takes drugs to mask pain, they are temporarily filled with euphoria and relief. Jesus' presence can often feel just like that, except it's not a temporary masking of pain or disappointment — He is the healer of it! Jesus is peace. He is security. He is love and validation even in the midst of painful and undesirable circumstances. *His presence has the supernatural power to satisfy and fulfill our core desires without the need of improved circumstances (or substances).*

But, as I keep saying, this is completely unnatural to us. That's why we need the transforming power of adversity. In the midst of hardship and pain, we have the opportunity to discover Jesus as Life when our circumstances have become the opposite of abundance. We must learn to seek and ask Jesus to give us His Life-giving presence without asking for improved circumstances and better outcomes. Yes, this will be hard! This requires intense transformation. It will take time and healing. It will also require that we seek the presence of Jesus more than we seek anything else under the sun. We must keep asking for His indwelling and transforming presence as if our life depends on Him, because it does.

He will show up, but usually not in the way nor the timing we would like. When He does, though, we are filled with peace and contentment that transcends all our natural understanding. His presence has the superhuman power to wash away all fear, pain, and discontent. He is the heavenly bread that satisfies our hunger. He is the springs of living water that quenches our thirst. He is the light that obliterates all darkness. He binds up our broken hearts and sets us free!

Jesus' presence is the promise of abundant Life He said He came to give us. He came to give Himself as the fullness of Life we so deeply desire. This is the ultimate point of Christianity, but it has been sadly missed by so many Christians. Most Christians pretty much only see Jesus as their Savior and a moral guide — which are wonderful gifts from God, to say the least. But sadly, few Christians discover Jesus as the fulfillment of their true desires. And so, *few find the path to Life that is Jesus Christ.*

Here's how important this is. Take notice of how sternly Jesus rebuked the religious leaders of His day (the Pharisees) for missing this Life-giving reality about Himself:

> *"You have your heads in your Bibles constantly because you think you'll find eternal life there. But you miss the forest for the trees. These Scriptures are all about me! And here I am, standing right before you,* **and you aren't willing to receive from me the life you say you want.**"

JOHN 5:39-40 (The Message)

Jesus is telling the Pharisees that He is the abundant Life they're looking for, but they're unwilling to accept this reality. He declares that all scripture reveals that He is the source of Life they desire — that we desire. But to some degree or another, we all do the same thing the Pharisees did: we seek substitutes to give us Life instead of seeking Jesus as Life — even when we're studying the Bible diligently!

Now, if this promise of *Life in Jesus* sounds disappointing to you, you're in good company. Again, it's not something that comes naturally to us. We've been conditioned from birth to believe happiness can be found in better outcomes and pleasant circumstances. So the idea that Jesus is the only true source of happiness doesn't quite align with our mindset and expectations. But, God already knows this far more than we do, and so, adversity is necessary to help us come to our senses, like the Prodigal Son did *in his hunger.* Only the wilderness of adversity can help us see how natural living keeps us from seeing Jesus as Life. And without adversity acting as a wake-up call, we will remain blindly committed to finding forms of satisfaction through our own efforts for the rest of our days.

Unfortunately, most people have resigned themselves to a life that is as pleasant as they can arrange for by their own wisdom and abilities. All the while the hunger in their hearts persist, or worse, rages more intensely into a runaway forest fire of sin. For many, the inner thirst gets so intense, they eventually give themselves over to destructive lifestyles or addictions to anesthetize the pain and discontent.

But those who discover the Life-giving reality of Jesus *redirect their natural inclinations for worldly results* to be satisfied in Him, regardless of their circumstances. They seek true peace, security, and joy in the presence of Jesus that better outcomes and pleasant circumstances can never give. As an example of this uncommon approach to life, I want to revisit an astounding revelation from the Apostle Paul, which I previously mentioned:

> *"I have learned the secret of being content in any and every situation … whether living in plenty or in want."*

PHILIPPIANS 4:12 (NIV)

This statement is incredible! This isn't how we naturally approach life. As I asked before, aren't we naturally content when we have plenty, but *dis*content when we are in want? Paul is revealing a new paradigm of the good news of the Gospel, of Life to the full. Let me unpack a few hidden gems in this verse that reveal the secret Paul found for himself.

First, I believe contentment is the sum of our truest desires (our seven core needs) — to be happy, secure, at peace, loved, validated, and living meaningful lives in healthy relationships. To be truly content is to have these needs fulfilled and complete in our lives without fear or doubt. Abundant Life is true contentment, which is what we all want more than anything in this life — and Paul declared that he learned this secret way to live.

Second, many other passages of Paul's writings reveal that the secret of his contentment is in Jesus, not his circumstances, because his circumstances often left him in great adversity and severe want. When we are in want, or things are bad, our human nature is to feel discontent because God did not create us to live in a broken world. But the Life-giving presence of Jesus can cause us to be fully content regardless of our lack or want — even in pain. This can only happen *supernaturally*, because nothing in this world has the power to truly satisfy. That's why Paul said:

> *"But whatever were gains to me I now consider loss for the sake of Christ. What is more, I consider everything a loss because of the surpassing worth of knowing Christ Jesus my Lord, for whose sake I have lost all things. I consider them garbage, that I may gain Christ…"*

PHILIPPIANS 3:7-8 (NIV)

I'll be honest, I used to view this verse with a bit of disdain. It felt like the Apostle Paul was saying lofty things like this just to sound hyper-spiritual. It bugged me. But now I get it. Now I understand how he truly discovered Jesus to be the Life-giving spirit that is worth giving up all the counterfeits he had once believed would give him the Life he desired. He came to see how anything apart from Jesus was a losing proposition. Everything apart from Jesus was worthless trash.

Therefore, God's ultimate good for us is to reveal the reality that Jesus is the Life we desire, even when He doesn't fix our broken or painful circumstances. God must use the scarcity and pain of the wilderness of adversity to wean us from our natural expectations and drivenness for better circumstances. He then waits, sometimes in excruciating silence, for us to surrender our natural expectations. Our loving, heavenly Father waits until we've put our natural sufficiencies to death — *by our own free will* — so that His supernatural abundance can fill us into overflowing through Jesus Christ.

Jesus' nature is Life-giving. It's what He kept saying about Himself the entire time He was here on earth. We can only receive this Life-giving realty when we put our complete faith in Jesus, and nothing else. Today, He offers the very thing we are all seeking. He is the fulfillment of our true desires — Life to the full! All we have to do is surrender to His hidden path of Life and He will satisfy us in a way the world cannot. Consider Jesus' own words in the following passages:

> *"It is the Spirit who gives life; the flesh profits nothing; the words that I have spoken to you are spirit and are life."*

JOHN 6:63 (NASB)

> *Jesus said, "Everyone who drinks this water will get thirsty again and again. Anyone who drinks the water I give will never thirst — not ever. The water I give will be an artesian spring within, gushing fountains of endless life."*

JOHN 4:13-14 (The Message)

> *"I am the bread of life; he who comes to Me will not hunger, and he who believes in Me will never thirst."*

JOHN 6:35 (NASB)

Until we are willing to surrender to God's hidden path to Life, we will languish in our insatiable thirst and hunger. And until we believe Jesus is our true Life, we will never find what we are truly after here under the sun.

"For the gate is small and the way is narrow that leads to life, and there are few who find it."

MATTHEW 7:14 (NASB)

"For whoever wishes to save his life will lose it; but whoever loses his life for My sake (to gain Me) will find it."

MATTHEW 16:25 (NASB)

"In Him was life, and that life was the light of all mankind."

JOHN 1:4 (NIV)

These amazing verses point to a reality few find, even though everyone is seeking abundant Life every second of their lives. The Bible proclaims that *Jesus is abundant Life!* He is the only source of true and lasting love, happiness, peace, and security. Therefore, we must seek Him with everything we've got instead of anything here under the sun.

Jesus is peace. He is security. He is love and validation even in the midst of painful and undesirable circumstances.

RECEIVING GOD'S LIFE-GIVING PLEASURE

You've heard me share several stories of God's rescue in the midst of our wilderness. These experiences of God's provision from His heavenly realm were exhilarating, to say the least, but like all things under the sun, the provision was still fleeting. It wasn't everlasting because everything in our fleshly realm is temporal — even if God gives it. However, Kim and I made sure that our faith and view of God would not be short-lived and fade away into the busyness of life once we came out of each wilderness experience. We stayed close to Jesus, even in the natural abundance we were experiencing. We were learning to abide in the Life-giving spirit of Jesus in deeper and deeper ways.

> *"Abide in Me, and I in you. As the branch cannot bear fruit of itself unless it abides in the vine, so neither can you unless you abide in Me ... If you abide in Me, and My words abide in you, ask whatever you wish, and it will be done for you."*

John 15:4 & 7 (NASB)

Now, this last part trips up a lot of people. It simply sounds too good to be true. I challenge you to admit you've tried asking for whatever you wish, and nothing happened, right? I must confess I have. But Kim and I have been working hard to apply the lessons we've learned so far. We've discover that abiding in Jesus means that we align our needs and desires with His Life-giving reality — His complete and abundant goodness towards us. This further means, that we bring our expectations for outcomes to God to be fulfilled according to the good He has stored up for us in His heavenly realm.

We continue to train ourselves to see difficulties and struggles as an opportunity to see God show up with His solutions and His provisions. This means that when we ask for whatever we wish, it will come from whatever good God has for us, because He's a good father, and we are His favored sons and daughters.

And so, when the pandemic hit in 2020, our hearts were ready for anything. And sure enough, I went the first 8 months of that year with no new income. Yeah, we weren't happy about that, but we also weren't afraid. By now, we understood that God wanted to show up in our lives in His supernatural ways. One big reality about God that we'd learned in our adversities (of many to be sure) was that God is just itching to do miracles in our lives. He longs to do miracles in yours too. The problem is that the kind of circumstances that require miracles are often frightening to us. And fear only steals, kills, and destroys.

So, here's another miracle God gave us that will blow your mind — it blows everyone's mind who hears it. You see, our daughter Sydney was supposed to start her freshman year of college in August of 2020. But having gone 8 months with no new income, it had become uncertain how we were going to pay for it. So Kim and I did what we had learned to do: just go to God with His favorite request.

"Father, what do you have for us?"

We asked God for whatever good gift He had in store for us, like any good father does. We didn't tell Him what to do. We simply trusted that He was good and had our best in mind, no matter how things played out. And once we gave it over to God, we disciplined our hearts and minds to stay focused on the Life-giving presence of Jesus, rather than being consumed by anxiety and the natural perception of our lack.

One week later we received a letter in the mail from Nokia, the large telecom company, asking Kim to contact them about her pension. I immediately believed it was a scam because Kim had never worked for Nokia. What we didn't know, was that Nokia had bought Lucent Technologies back in 2015. What we also didn't know, was that Lucent Technologies had automatic enrollment in their pension program for all employees on their fifth year of employment. And what you need to know is that Kim had quit Lucent Technologies way back in 2000 after working there for 13 years. To do the math for you, she hadn't worked for Lucent in 20 years. And all this time, we had no clue whatsoever she had been enrolled in a pension — none!

So, to our astonishment, the lady at Nokia informed us that Kim had $42,000 sitting in a pension account in her name! She just wanted to know where to send the check. For 20 years there had been no communication to us about this money — none at all — until just when we needed it. God had done it again! And He didn't just provide for the first semester of Sydney's college. This amount of money covered her entire four-year undergraduate program!

Now, you may be thinking, *"Hang on Mark! I thought it wasn't about better outcomes, pleasant circumstances, and positive results here under the sun? This sure sounds like that."*

You see, none of our miracles came as a result of *our* efforts, wisdom, or strategies. We know this for a fact because I had been trying to land work as hard as I could during all those lean years, but my efforts were mostly unsuccessful. Yet the provisions that poured in were clearly God-given because none of it came from *our* doing. It was simply given to us by God to satisfy our worldly needs from His heavenly realm in His inconceivable ways and timing. That's why Jesus informed us that we simply don't need to be afraid in times of trouble. Instead, He's ready to give us the desires of our heart in the midst of any adversity, as we seek Him for Life in all circumstances!

> *"Peace I leave with you; My peace I give you. I do not give to you as the world gives. Do not let your hearts be troubled and do not be afraid."*

JOHN 14:27 (NIV)

Yet, there was something even greater than miraculous architecture work and hidden pension money that God released from heaven in all of this: He gifted me the revelation of the message in this book. You see, during the course of the past 30 years of my life, I have been seeking to understand the truest value of God more than anything else in my life. I've learned much, but every great revelation I had previously received from God only led to another question (or fifty). My wilderness experiences strengthened my resolve to receive more understanding and revelation, for I knew I wouldn't survive these difficult adversities without them.

However, knowledge, no matter how godly, offers no relief for the thirst of our souls. And so, my thirst only became more and more intense because I had no satisfying outcomes or pleasant circumstances to keep me comfortably numb. So, when God showed up in 2017 with the bounty of work described in chapter 3, He also gave me the most spiritual revelation and clarity I've ever had. This gift of revelation included Jesus' Life-giving reality like I'd never experienced before! I came to understand what the missionary and Olympiad Eric Liddle said about running. He said: *"When I run, I feel God's pleasure."* Kim and I have been experiencing God's pleasure *through our adversity!*

I share these stories to encourage you that God has the same amazing miracles in store for you as well. Remember, it's God's desire to bless His creation. But He needs us to discover the Life-giving gift of Jesus Christ *before* we are able to properly receive His circumstantial gifts. So if you want to experience God's miracles on a regular basis, you will first have to be transformed into the kind of person who is filled with the spring of living water, which is Jesus. Here's what this looks like for me.

DRINKING JESUS

During the darkest hours of my adversity I kept asking Jesus, *"If you are living water then how do I "drink You?" How do I get your Life-giving reality?"* It turns out there was nothing I could do except continue walking the path I believed He had for me by seeking Him with all my heart, soul, mind and strength — *and* believing in Him more than in my difficult circumstances. I discovered that God's command of total surrender comes with the same extraordinary promise He gave the Israelites when they were in the ultimate adversity of enslavement to the Babylonians:

> *"Then you will call on me and come and pray to me, and I will listen to you. You will seek me and find me* **when you seek me with all your heart**. *I will be found by you," declares the Lord…"*

JEREMIAH 29:12 (TNIV)

All I could do to gain the thirst-quenching promise of Jesus was to keep walking by faith the dry and barren path I believed God had for me. I had to keep seeking Jesus as Life with all my heart, even though my heart intensely ached for circumstantial relief. My main responsibility was to resist my fleshly impulses to secure any kind of alleviation through whatever outcomes I could arrange or secure.

Only when our hearts are drained of its self-sufficient efforts to find Life through outcomes under the sun can we truly seek God with all our hearts. Only when we've given up on the natural results the world offers to secure happiness will we discover God's lavish joy to bless us supernaturally. Until then, we are double-minded. We are conflicted in our hearts.

To the extent that we seek anything other than Jesus for Life, we are stiff-arming God and His heavenly promise to satisfy us the way He designed us in the first place. Any fulfillment we seek apart from Jesus is sin, and results in spiritual and emotional death. The Apostle James warned us of this conflict:

> *"Come near to God and he will come near to you. Wash your hands, you sinners, and purify your hearts, you double-minded … Humble yourselves before the Lord, and he will lift you up."*

JAMES 4:8 & 10 (TNIV)

The problem is, we can't drink Jesus as Life. We don't have that ability. Instead, He pours Himself into our hearts when the work of surrender has been completed. We can only humble ourselves in faithful obedience before the One who is the only satisfaction of our heart's desires. Only then will our hearts and minds be purely and singularly aligned with God's life-giving source. Only then will we drink of the Spring of Living Water, which is Jesus.

I'll offer some practical ways I continue to receive God's spring of living water, in Chapter 9. But for now, there's one more purpose why God leads His children into the wilderness of adversity and causes them to hunger. The lessons of the wilderness conclude with a very pleasing promise — one that many Christians don't even know is available, or have outright dismissed. It's the final secret of adversity found in Deuteronomy 8.

If we sow into the world's system, then we will only reap outcomes under the sun which cannot give Life. But if we sow into God's unseen kingdom by faith, then we will reap His Life-giving goodness.

CHAPTER 8

SECRET #7: GOD'S LIFE-GIVING PROSPERITY

"But you shall [earnestly] remember the Lord your God, for it is He who gives you power to get wealth ..."

DEUTERONOMY 8:18 (AMPC)

FREEDOM UNDER THE SUN

*C*an you believe this verse is actually in the Bible? It's a promise God made to His people on multiple occasions. One of the most famous verses in the Bible confirms this offer:

"I know what I'm doing. I have it all planned out — plans to take care of you, not abandon you, plans to give you the future you hope for."

Jeremiah 29:11 (The Message)

God has plans for us to "get wealth" so that we don't have to sweat and toil through our own efforts and strength! This means that God gives provision and success in unnatural ways that align with our purpose and design. This isn't only about financial wealth, though. In fact, most often the wealth God gives us has very little to do with money. He may give a person great influence, like Joseph, who was raised up to the highest power over all commerce of Egypt. He gave Abraham the wealth of offspring. He gave the apostles and Billy Graham (and many other evangelists) the wealth of preaching and spreading the Gospel. There are many stories of doctors, scientists, artists, politicians, inventors, and regular folk who achieved great and world-changing success as a blessing from God due to their total commitment to His Life-giving reality. As we surrender our expectations and outcomes to God, He will:

> *"… do immeasurably more than all we ask or imagine, according to His power that is at work within us…"*

EPHESIANS 3:20 (NIV)

This doesn't mean we sit back and do nothing, expecting money, success, or prosperity to fall from the sky. *That's nonsense!* And it's ungodly. It means we must connect with God and His heavenly reality which is always within reach. We must seek the presence of Jesus with everything we've got — with all our heart, soul, mind, and strength — *to discover Jesus as our source of Life* — as our ultimate source of joy, peace, security, love, meaning, and validation in this life.

Only when we become free of our natural addictions to better outcomes and pleasant circumstances, will we be able to receive the heavenly prosperity He has for us. God will then give us success and prosperity that will set us free from striving in our own strength and wisdom as we live in this world. His promise to show us how to get wealth requires that we first be set free from self-sufficiency and self-reliance. Otherwise, we risk becoming further addicted to money, success, or leisure. Again, this is not a "Prosperity Gospel!" It's *God's own promise* to lavishly bless those who live fully committed to His unseen reality, because it's His desire to do so.

God's been abundantly clear about this:

> *"Study this Book of Instruction continually. Meditate on it day and night so you will be sure to obey everything written in it. Only then will you prosper and succeed in all you do."*

JOSHUA 1:8 (NLT)

Notice how generous God's offer of the promised land is to His chosen people in Deuteronomy. If you are born again, the following promise is for you as well:

> *"For the Lord your God is bringing you into a good land … a land in which you will eat bread without scarcity, in which you will lack nothing."*

DEUTERONOMY 8:7 & 9 (NKJV)

Only when we become free of our natural addictions to better outcomes and pleasant circumstances, we will be able to receive the prosperity God has for us.

God's core desire is to satisfy our core desires. That's why He made us.

God didn't create us to survive on our own. He didn't make us to live from our own strengths and wisdom. In fact, self-sufficiency and self-reliance is the root of all sin. We must live with a daily understanding that *our flesh profits nothing!* We can choose to live life from our own strength, but it will *never* get us what we truly want. Instead, He created us to live without scarcity and lack through His Life-giving presence.

The curse of self-reliance has everyone seeking Life with everything they've got, but from the wrong sources. The laziest freeloader is seeking Life just as hard as those intensely driven by greed, as well as everyone one else in between these two extremes! So is the moralist and the hedonist. Even if we gain a genuine and committed belief in God, we are still infected with this drive to find Life through our own efforts and wisdom. Instead, God has repeatedly promised to bless us with the very thing we desire. Notice the amazing offer God makes at the end of this verse:

> *"Come, all you who are thirsty, come to the waters; and you who have no money, come, buy and eat! Come, buy wine and milk without money and without cost. Why spend money on what is not bread, and your labor on what does not satisfy? Listen, listen to me, and eat what is good, and you will delight in the richest of fare. Give ear and come to me; listen, **that you may live.**"*

ISAIAH 55:1-3 (NIV)

JESUS IS LIFE!

You see? It's not about money. God doesn't need money to give you a prosperous life. *He is abundant Life.* He gives Himself, which fills us with happiness, peace, love and purpose. God wants to give us abundant Life because He made us for it. *That's why it hurts so bad not to have it!*

Abundant life in Jesus is what we all want. This is what we chase after and hope for all the days of our lives. It turns out God wants this for us too. But we've gotten our view of Life and God all mixed up. Since our first breath, we've been misled into believing the greatest lie of all time — *that we can find Life on our own, by our own efforts and wisdom.*

In addition, God has made each person unique in order that each of us may offer something great and wonderful to the world. Therefore, as we surrender to His hidden path through the wilderness of adversity, He will begin to reveal our unique purpose and prosperity in ways we could never imagine. Here are a few more verses that reveal God's prosperity promise.

"The kingdom of heaven is like treasure hidden in a field. When a man found it, he hid it again, and then in his joy went and sold all he had and bought that field."

MATTHEW 13:44 (NIV)

"I will give you hidden treasures, riches stored in secret places, so that you may know that I am the Lord, the God of Israel, who summons you by name."

ISAIAH 45:3 (NIV)

"Trust in the Lord and do good. Then you will live safely in the land and prosper."

PSALMS 37:3 (NLT)

As we surrender to His hidden path through the wilderness of adversity, He will begin to reveal our unique purpose and prosperity in ways we could never imagine.

ALIGNING WITH GOD FOR TRUE WEALTH

In the three years leading up to the housing market collapse (2005 —2007), I made more money than I expected. Of course, it was due to a monster housing "bubble" giving me false prosperity. The money I made due to the bubble and the ensuing loss of money once the bubble burst, were all a result of "sowing and reaping" in that broken system. To be clear, I wasn't working sinfully or selfishly. In fact, I was seeking God's ways in every decision and transaction I made. My point here is to contrast how my wealth during those three years was simply an outcome of a worldly system rather than from God's heavenly reality.

Since then, I've learned to "sow and reap" a different way, as described beautifully in this amazing paraphrase of the famous

Matthew 6:33 passage. Here, Jesus instructs us how to view our lack or pain:

> *"People who don't know God and the way he works fuss over these things, but you know both God and how he works. Steep your life in God-reality, God-initiative, God-provisions. Don't worry about missing out. You'll find all your everyday human concerns will be met. Give your entire attention to what God is doing right now, and don't get worked up about what may or may not happen tomorrow. God will help you deal with whatever hard things come up when the time comes."*

MATTHEW 6:32-34 (The Message)

I now live my life and run my businesses *"steeped in God-reality."* This means several things to me:

1. I always ask God that I may receive only that which He has for me, in all situations, from the belief that I'm His loved and favored son — because that's what I am.

2. Before I meet a new potential client, I always ask God that I may receive only that which He has for me. After I have met the potential client, I always align my outcome expectations in prayer to whatever God has in store for me. I do this without envisioning any outcome (like hoping for a signed contract and design deposit) because I only need to envision God's goodness — which is more real than anything else.

3. Whenever I experience trouble of any kind (especially with work related issues), I've learned to immediately ask Jesus for His overcoming power to replace any trouble with His promise of peace, as He taught us in John 16:33. (By the way, visit my website at www.HiddenPath.Life for a lot more on this amazing verse.) Again, I purposefully do not envision any desired

outcome or solution regarding the problem I'm facing. Rather, I focus my heart on the promise of peace Jesus says is available in Him. I've experienced many amazing miracles doing this in all areas of life!

4. I don't run my business from a view of need or lack — *even if I have them* — because all that does is stir up my natural energies and emotions of "make-it-happen" self-sufficiency. Instead, I run my business from my true desires according to the words and directions God has given me. This allows me to live free from being controlled by scarcity, or any need for security or validation through my work. However, please don't think I do this perfectly. I still get caught up in the emotions of negative experiences. But I'm getting quicker and quicker in going from fear to faith in every challenge and hardship.

5. Whenever I find that I've let my flesh lead me into self-sufficiency and self-reliance, and therefore suffer the natural consequences of doing so (such as worry, striving, or other negative feelings), I'm quick to sincerely repent. And I take my time with this. There's no repentance "drive-thru" with God because that's not true repentance after all. True restorative repentance requires coming back to God and His heavenly reality by first surrendering and rejecting all other natural strategies to which I've turned. As soon as I realize I've been operating in fleshly ways, I stop everything I'm doing and sit with God in honest and sincere meditation. Busyness is one of the most common obstacles to finding abundant Life. So, I'll stay in relational prayer to receive His Life-giving presence, while I do what's before me to do in any situation.

GOD'S WEALTH-GENERATING REVELATIONS

Throughout the course of the past 13 years of my financial adversities, God has revealed two wealth-generating strategies. During my adversities, God would activate these wealth-generating blessings *just when I needed them.* They were part of His "architectural manna" to show me that I could believe in Him more than my circumstances — which is His ultimate goal in our trouble and distress. Today, they enhance my businesses far beyond my expectations.

Again, you may be thinking, *"Hang on, Mark! How were these wealth-generating revelations of any use if they didn't take you out of your financial wilderness — you know, make you rich?"*

That's a reasonable question. But it's just that: human reason. You see, God's desire is that we see things completely different from how we humanly see things. God's desire is that we see *Him* as our true wealth; not more money, or landing that big promotion, or whatever better outcome we'd like to experience.

If I had been consumed with finding better financial outcomes during the Great Recession in order to simply cobble together any number of jobs necessary to pay the bills, then I most likely would not have been in the right frame of mind and heart to receive God's rhema words. Had I sought my own path in my adversity, I would not have been in the place God needed me to be to experience the following life-changing revelations and divine appointments, which He used to make ends meet for us. In fact, these business strategies helped us pay our bills in much more enjoyable ways than working two or three random jobs in the

Everything we were made for — to live a full and abundant Life with God — hangs in the balance.

We must believe and seek this unseen reality as if our life depends on it, because it does!

midst of a terrible job shortage. The path of believing in God more than my own logic and reason *paid off* — literally! Here's what God revealed in the midst of my wilderness:

Best 3D in my industry

At the beginning of the Great Recession in 2008, Jiri, a young, hardworking immigrant from the Czech Republic was laid off from a struggling framing crew in Atlanta, Georgia (where I live and work). I didn't know him at that time, but one of his last jobs was framing a large home I had designed. A few months later he called a meeting with me and my business partner Lee (who was the builder of the home Jiri had been framing). He wanted us to see something he created for us.

Lee and I agreed to meet Jiri at the construction site of this particular home. He plopped his laptop down on a stack of plywood just outside the partially built garage and showed us a mind-blowing 3D rendering he had created of that same house. Our jaws dropped! It turned out, that after loosing his framing job, Jiri had taught himself how to create some of the best 3D visualization in the residential industry.

To make a long story short, Lee, Jiri, and I immediately formed an architectural 3D services partnership. Since then, Jiri has perfected a 3D residential solution which is second-to-none in the housing market. It has allowed all of us to capture very high-end clients who are willing to pay much higher fees because they want to see their designs at the level that our 3D services offer.

Furthermore, during the remainder of the Great Recession, Lee and I would find ourselves as one of dozens of other design-build teams competing for the few available custom home projects. Our

3D services gave us a huge edge over our competitors, allowing us to secure far more contracts than we otherwise would have gained without these services. Jiri was a direct part of God's financial salvation for me and my family, and for Lee and his family during the Great Recession. But here's what's really interesting about this wealth-generating solution of God's: Jiri is an atheist! (And I share all this with his permission, by the way.)

I know this amazing "gift of 3D" was given to me from God because I did *nothing* to make it happen. Plus, it was what God revealed to us as a significant differentiator to potential clients, in order to gain work we never would have won otherwise. This was God's provision-plan to sustain us throughout the dark days of the Recession. It didn't make us rich. Rather it provided exactly what we needed, when we needed it. It was like the Israelites receiving heavenly food in a barren environment. Like Joseph receiving favor from his captors. And like Naomi and Ruth being accepted into Boaz's family. It wasn't where any of them (or us) wanted to be, however God provided supernaturally *in the midst* of their adversity (and ours).

We have to get this! God rarely removes people from their difficult circumstances. However, God is *always* willing to bless His children as He walks with us *through* our wilderness journeys. God's desire is to release miracles in the midst of hardship and pain to show us how to walk with Him in it, rather than expect or demand that He remove us from it. He seeks a relationship of belief in Him, rather than belief in His power alone.

Divine appointment with an info marketer

Right about the same time I had met Jiri, I met Kris. Kris was in the same financial free fall as I was due to the Great Recession. His business was selling a series of courses he created to "flip homes," which was immensely popular and successful throughout the years leading up to the housing and credit market collapse. We met at a men's retreat and hit it off due to our similar industry and financial struggles.

Kris had no work at all, as his industry would be entirely shut down for the next five to six years. So, he and I spent a lot of time together at our local Starbucks. There, he taught me about an emerging and little-known industry called "Information Marketing." The basis of this industry offers in-depth solutions to problems and mistakes inherent to any service or skill, usually in the form of a manual or a course. This idea immediately sparked a revelation in my heart and mind.

You see, the industry of designing and building custom homes is full of pitfalls and problems that can become a financial nightmare for homeowners. From cost overruns to missed expectations, Lee (my builder-partner from the previous story) and I had heard them all. We didn't operate our services that way, but we were fully aware of the mistakes so many other architects and builders make in our industry. Kris's info-marketing guidance helped me write a 250-page course that teaches homeowners how to avoid common pitfalls, find the right architect and builder, and design and build their dream home on time, on budget, with no costly surprises.

This informational tool gave Lee and me instant credibility with potential clients. This custom home guide book, coupled with the 3D services, gave us a marketing "secret weapon" like nothing else in the custom home industry!

God divinely appointed and revealed these powerful services to us, which He used as the conduits for our miraculous survival of the worst industry collapse since the Great Depression. Without them, we most likely would have lost our businesses and our homes, and become victims of that devastating economic tsunami. Today, Lee and I continue to operate and succeed at the top of our industry because of these gifts from God. These gifts were freely given to me from God's heavenly realm when I needed them the most — when my strength and wisdom were incapable of overcoming my adversity.

God wants to do the same for all his creation. However, He desires a relationship with His children — a relationship of belief and trust that will feel very much like being called out of our comfort zones, and into the frightening scarcity of the wilderness we are trying to avoid. God's loving goal for us is total surrender and complete dependence on Him. This is most often terrifying to us because it's completely contrary and unnatural for us to do. But trust me, God's heavenly outcomes are worth it!

RECEIVING GOD'S PROSPERITY

Those who are willing to believe in God more than they believe in their circumstances will see Him begin to do things beyond human imaginations. He most likely won't remove our adversity, in order to show us far deeper and transforming goodness than better outcomes and pleasant circumstances can ever offer. This is why we must all learn to walk the hidden path of adversity with God.

This hidden path also includes revelations and provisions of God's Life-giving prosperity *while* we live in a world that cannot give true and lasting satisfaction. We must seek God's unnatural ways that offer the great good of abundant Life we desire. If we don't, we will remain enslaved to self-reliance and discontent. If we seek "the comfortable life" in this world through our own wisdom and strategies — even with a commitment to godliness along with it — we will miss the greater good God has for us. We will miss the prosperity of God.

This prosperity from God is a real thing— *but it's not about money!* Though it may sometimes involve some, God's prosperity always results in the satisfaction of our true desires according to how God made us. This is revealed all throughout His scriptures: God lavishly blesses those who are willing to believe in Him more than in their natural circumstances here under the sun.

THIS IS NOT "PROSPERITY GOSPEL!"

I want to be abundantly clear: I am not pushing a Prosperity Gospel! *The one true Gospel is that **only Jesus** is the fulfillment of our desires, even when we are in want.* To seek the outcome of wealth in order to quench the thirst in our hearts will only result in futile and fleeting pleasures under the sun which cannot give Life. The Bible unequivocally calls this death. We must push past our natural human addiction for temporal security through wealth and the futile validation of success. No great worldly achievement will ever satisfy the thirst in our hearts and the hunger in our souls because God made us to be satisfied only in Him.

Yet God *does* bless His children materially all throughout the Bible, and He has blessed me and many others I know as well. *We cannot force God into a box that neither excludes nor compels Him to do material things on our behalf.* The Bible has scores of examples of God blessing people financially, relationally, and physically. When it comes to these human currencies, our responsibility is to surrender our will and desires to Jesus, believing in Him as the only source of true satisfaction and fulfillment. We must remain in a posture of receiving whatever God has for us — be it in plenty or in want. This is the hidden path Jesus said few find. This is the path to abundant Life.

We cannot force God into a box that neither excludes nor compels Him to do material things on our behalf.

AN IMPORTANT CAUTION!

This promise to receive God's wealth-getting revelation has a foolproof "safety mechanism" to it. If our underlying motivation for seeking God is to gain happiness, peace, and security through worldly wealth, we immediately forfeit access to God's wealth-getting offer made in Deuteronomy 8:18. This happens because the moment the object of our heart's affections is primarily on getting wealth, the thirst of our heart becomes captivated on the world's system rather than on God's heavenly reality. At that moment, our sufficiency is centered on outcomes and results of this world which is subject to the spiritual law that we reap what we sow. If we sow into the world's system to get Life, then we will only reap outcomes under the sun which cannot give Life. But if we sow into God's unseen kingdom through surrender and faith to gain *His presence*, then we will reap His Life-giving goodness, which includes His power to get wealth.

I trip this safety mechanism of God's wealth promise all the time! So often, my flesh will draw my emotions and desires back into the "Dark Side" of self-sufficiency and self-protection. I'll chase a business or ministry opportunity that seems right to me, but in the end, after a lot of sweat and toil, it results in a costly waste of time and resources. The only thing for me to do is to repent from abiding in my own wisdom, rather than abiding more closely with the Life-giving Spirit that is Jesus.

We must fiercely discern and expose the motivations of our heart! Like David, we must ask God to root out anything that can disqualify us from gaining His intended good for us.

> *"Search me, O God, and know my heart; test me and know my anxious thoughts. See if there is any hurtful way in me, and lead me along the path of everlasting life."*

PSALMS 139:23-24 (NASB)

> *"Don't be misled: No one makes a fool of God. What a person plants, he will harvest. The person who plants selfishness, ignoring the needs of others — ignoring God — harvests a crop of weeds. All he'll have to show for his life is weeds! But the one who plants in*

response to God, letting God's Spirit do the growth work in him, harvests a crop of real life, eternal life."

GALATIANS 6:7-8 (The Message)

So, let's find this path! Let's find this Life-giving realty of Jesus! In this next chapter, I reveal a secret weapon to finding Jesus as the Life *and prosperity* we all seek.

CHAPTER 9

DAVID'S SECRET: HOW TO FIND THE PATH TO LIFE

"You make known to me the path of life ..."

PSALMS 16:11 (NIV)

SEEK THE HIDDEN PATH

Prosperity comes either from our own efforts to secure it through the system of the world, or we receive it from God and His heavenly realm. When we seek prosperity by our own strategies and wisdom, it is cursed by the fleeting and Lifeless reality of all things under the sun. None of it will give us true and lasting Life because *only Jesus is Life.*

This promise of abundant Life cannot be earned or deserved. It can only be freely received by believing in, trusting in, and committing ourselves fully to Jesus Christ. We must believe He is good and has good for us. When adversity comes to us, we must follow His lead through the wilderness in full surrender. We must persevere and not give up as we are humbled, tested, and transformed into His children.

Only then are we able to receive true Life from our good and loving Father. Until we are willing to surrender to God's hidden path to Life, we will languish in our insatiable thirst and hunger. And until we believe Jesus is our true Life, we will never find what we are truly after here under the sun — because what we're *really after* isn't in any of the things we're after. We must seek Jesus and His Life-giving presence more than anything else in life. This is what David meant when he urged us to "delight in the Lord." He came to the point where he valued and desired nothing more than the presence of God.

> *Delight yourself in the LORD;*
> *and He will give you the desires of your heart.*

PSALMS 37:4 (NASB)

If we persevere in belief and faith in the Life-giving reality of Jesus — no matter what comes at us — He *will* lead us to the fulfillment of our desires. God's truest desire is to give us the desires of our heart — He created us for that in the first place! It has been His intention all along. God's ultimate blessing is to prosper us with peace, security, love, and joy in His presence. This is the rest from striving God promised in Exodus 33:14 (NIV):

> *The LORD replied, "My Presence will go with you,*
> *and I will give you rest."*

God's ultimate blessing is to prosper you with peace, security, love, and joy in His presence. This is the rest from striving God promised.

People work so hard to get to the point where they don't have to worry about their needs. Their true and God-given desire is to be at rest, but the system of this world does not cooperate with that outcome. It never has, and never will. Supernatural rest is God's offer to those who live by faith in His Life-giving promise. When God promises rest, He offers His presence that causes us to know with full confidence that our desires are fully met without lack, doubt, or fear of loss. *This is true prosperity!* It's readily available to be received without effort by anyone who believes in God's gracious goodness. The purpose of the wilderness of adversity, and the hunger we experience in it, is to discover the Life of true rest in Jesus.

But the journey follows a path we wouldn't naturally choose — a path God hides in adversity, found only by those who are willing to surrender to His unnatural ways. And so, we must submit ourselves to the seven hidden purposes in adversity revealed in Deuteronomy 8. As we do, God then leads us to the very thing we desire the most — Life!

"Oh, how great is Your goodness, which You have laid up for those who fear You, which You have prepared for those who trust in You ... You hide them in the secret place of Your presence ..."

PSALMS 31:19-20 (NASB)

So, here's a quick summary of the seven purposes of adversity we've covered:

1. We must humble ourselves to the reality that we will never find true Life here under the sun.

2. We must commit ourselves to God as He tests our faith by removing things we've counted on for Life.

3. We must repent of our self-sufficient tendencies, in order to discover and live from our true desires in our new heart.

4. We must live from God's revealed words, rather than our own wisdom and strategies.

5. We must live as sons and daughters of God, willing to receive His discipline intended to lead us into a Life-giving relationship with Him.

6. We must believe and receive God's great good, which is beyond our imagination, because it comes from God's heavenly reality.

7. We then receive God's Life-giving prosperity to bless us without striving or toiling, to lack nothing all the days of our lives, and finally find rest in the Life-giving realty of Jesus.

We must seek this hidden path more than anything else. No other way will truly satisfy!

This is what the LORD says: "Stand at the crossroads and look; ask for the ancient paths, ask where the good way is, and walk in it, and you will find rest for your souls."

JEREMIAH 6:16 (TNIV)

"... those who seek the LORD lack no good thing."

PSALM 34:10 (NIV)

"The LORD is good to those who depend on him, to those who search for him."

LAMENTATIONS 3:35 (NLT)

And I love this one!

"You're blessed when you stay on course, walking steadily on the road revealed by GOD. You're blessed when you follow his directions, doing your best to find Him."

PSALM 119:1-2 (The Message)

When Jesus promises rest, He offers His presence that causes us to know with full confidence that our desires are fully met without lack, doubt, or fear of loss. This is true prosperity!

HOW JESUS IS LIFE TO ME

I now live by faith in the realty that Jesus is my abundant Life, regardless of my circumstances or outcomes. As Paul so powerfully revealed in Philippians 1:17:

"… to live is Christ …"

This verse never made any real sense to me until I received the revelation of Christ's abundant Life reality in 2017. Paul's words sounded unreal. Again, it came across like the Apostle was trying to sound "super spiritual," but he wasn't offering something that was practical and livable. Now, I know that *Christ is my Life!* Being filled with this divine revelation has changed everything for me. I used to live every minute of my day seeking and arranging for better outcomes and positive results in everything I did. Now, I see the better way. The way of abiding in the Life-giving presence of Jesus instead of chasing after outcomes that only leave me exhausted and empty.

I don't always get it right. I still get caught up in trying to make the best of this crazy unpredictable world we all live in. But now I intentionally strive — *on a daily basis* — to live for the presence of Jesus as the only fulfilling source there is in life. My growing awareness of the Life-giving nature of Jesus helps me reject all my natural energies to arrange for the better outcomes I previously hoped would give me Life. Instead, I do whatever it takes, however long it takes, to abide in the presence of Jesus through prayer, studying the scriptures, and worshipfully meditating on the Life-giving reality of Jesus through surrender and repentance.

Now don't get me wrong, if I experience better outcomes and pleasant circumstances, I certainly enjoy them! But I don't cling to them for Life, because the moment I do, they become a *"vapor and a breath, a chasing after the wind."* Instead, I allow the challenges of life to bring me to the place of delighting and abiding in Jesus more than in pleasant circumstances. This takes commitment. This requires belief.

However, I was only able to come to this place by fully surrendering myself to all that God has for me, especially accepting and surrendering to the wildernesses of adversity. This was hard for me — *excruciatingly hard!* In my adversities, I was so confused and frustrated with my circumstances. In fact, I was most upset with God and *His unnatural ways* in it all, as He so often felt aloof and uncaring towards me. Many times I informed God He was crazy for thinking we humans can understand His ways. But I was determined to believe in God's goodness more than any circumstance I found myself in — pleasant or painful.

MY SECRET WEAPON

Again, I don't want you to think that I live in some continuous abundant Life "bliss." No one does, because we still have our flesh, which generates that inescapable conflict with our Jesus-connected spirit inside us. I still have to fight against self-sufficiency and self-reliance in order to receive abundant Life — and then, I must continue to fight to sustain it. I've found a vitally important weapon in this battle against natural thinking that helps me maintain my connection to Jesus as much as possible. It's found in one of David's amazing "journal entries" in Psalm 16:5-11 (NIV):

"Lord, you alone are my portion and my cup; You make my lot secure. The boundary lines have fallen for me in pleasant places; surely I have a delightful inheritance. I will praise the Lord, who counsels me; even at night my heart instructs me. I keep my eyes always on the Lord. With Him at my right hand, I will not be shaken. Therefore, my heart is glad and my tongue rejoices; my body also will rest secure, because You will not abandon me to the realm of the dead, nor will You let your faithful one see decay. You make known to me the path of life; You will fill me with joy in Your presence, with eternal pleasures at Your right hand."

Let me break down this mind-blowing passage, verse by verse, to show you the practical power of this transformational message. This is how I use this passage to connect — *and reconnect* — my heart and mind to the promise of God's Life-giving reality for me.

◼ Verse 5a:

"Lord, you alone are my portion and my cup ..."

We all want our proverbial "cup" filled — our portion of Life that will satisfy the thirst of our heart. We all naturally seek it through outcomes under the sun, which Jesus warned, leads us down the heavily populated path to destruction. David learned that *only God embodies abundant Life*. Through my many years of adversity, I too learned this Life-giving reality — that apart from Christ I can do nothing, like Jesus warned in John 15:5! So, I train my heart and mind on a daily basis to continuously connect to the fact that *God alone* is my full portion and cup of satisfaction. Most mornings as I'm waking up, before I even get out of bed, I will ask Jesus to fill me with His Life-giving reality for the day. I don't do it as ritual. I do it as a necessity of my reality on earth. I do it because I now know that my happiness, peace, and security come from Him.

■ Verse 5b - 6:

"... You make my lot secure. The boundary lines have fallen for me in pleasant places ..."

This passage has powerful meaning to me as an architect. I start every design project by requiring each client to secure a boundary survey of their lot (the word "lot" is an industry term for property). This is an important document because it reveals the legal extents of property ownership on which I can design my client's new home. It also tells me what's out of bounds — what's beyond the owner's right to build on.

This Psalm helps me envision a spiritual "lot" that God has granted me — *a pleasant, enduring, heavenly and Life-giving outcome.* No one can take it from me. Nothing can diminish or destroy it. And I can only receive it by faith in God, believing in His great love for me.

Furthermore, when I visualize this "lot" of pleasant outcomes God has for me, I intentionally do not envision any specific outcomes or circumstances that I prefer or desire. Instead, I imagine God's goodness for me as being so great that I will love whatever He gives me. I've come to learn that God's outcomes are far better than my own, so I intentionally resist my natural bent to visualize any particular outcome or result.

To this day, I still can't get over the fact that I designed the home of one of the most successful NFL players in the history of the league. I would never have imagined that outcome which was given to me by God. This is one inconceivable gift, of many, that I've received from God. This has taught me to intentionally leave my expectations of His provisions blank, as an act of belief, faith, and submission to His great goodness. And so, I intentionally resist my natural tendency to visualize outcomes, and instead, I ask God for His lot for me.

■ Verse 7 - 8a:

> *"I will praise the Lord, who counsels me; even at night my heart instructs me. I keep my eyes always on the Lord."*

I've learned that to live life apart from God's revelation is futile, and only ends in disappointment and eventual self-destruction to some degree or another. I've learned to seek God's divine revelation in all matters — *and to hear His voice* — which gives me exactly what I need to know when God is ready to reveal it. Without God's words, I'm left to figure life out on my own — and I don't want to live that way anymore! I've been down that road of self-sufficiency and self-reliance long enough to know it's a dead end!

I've also learned that God will not do things the way I would do them. Therefore, when He speaks through His scriptures or by His Spirit in me (through His rhema words), I'm prepared for His instructions and directions *to sometimes seem foolish to me*. I've learned through my many experiences (and failures) with God, to discern and obey His words as Life-giving and true no matter how crazy and unnatural they seem to me.

■ Verse 8b - 10a:

> *"With Him at my right hand, I will not be shaken ... my heart is glad and my tongue rejoices ... my body also will rest secure ... because You will not abandon me ..."*

These words speak to the unshakable peace and security every human being wants. *We all want rest!* So, I declare these words on a regular basis as the truth of God which He has for me. Whenever a negative situation attempts to steal my peace, security, and rest, I know that I'm not on my own to deal with it. *God has a plan to overcome it.* All I have to do is go to Him immediately in confidence and belief, to receive whatever He has for me, because everything He has for me is abundantly good.

Again, I don't envision the outcomes I prefer out of my own logic and wisdom to make me happy. Rather, I focus on the person of Jesus as *my fullness of Life.* Don't get me wrong. I don't ignore uncomfortable situations or problems in my life — that's denial, and foolish. When trouble comes, I present my needs and wants to God, as we are instructed to do in Philippians 4:6. Yet I've trained myself to intentionally resist formulating any outcomes in my mind *that my heart will latch onto* that I believe would give me relief from my troubling situation. Instead, I've developed the habit of visualizing Jesus' presence as the fulfillment of any need I have at any given moment.

To be clear, this isn't some "kumbaya" escapism. This is how I invite the overcoming presence of Jesus into my troubles as I engage them without fear and anxiety. I don't ignore or avoid difficult situations, but rather I first invite the Life-giving presence of Jesus into my troubling circumstances as I deal with them as best I know how.

■ Verse 11a:

"You make known to me the path of life ..."

This is such a powerful statement! I now know that all my adversities have been leading me to understand this life-changing reality in a tangible way. It took me a long time to get it, but know I know in the deepest part of my heart that it is impossible for me to find the path that leads to Life without God's intimate revelations. And so, I focus my heart, mind, and emotions on the invisible reality that *God reveals what I need to know and what I need to receive in order to have abundant Life.* Therefore, I don't have to worry about figuring it out. I don't have to strive, sweat, and toil to secure Life. Only God can do it, and it's His great desire to do so — *because His creation intention was to fill me with Life through His presence in the first place. It still is today!*

■ Verse 11b:

"... You will fill me with joy in Your presence, with eternal pleasures at Your right hand." (v. 11b)

Yes! This is what we all want — never-ending joy and pleasures! And it's only found in God's Life-giving presence. I constantly proclaim this to my heart and mind in order to override all the natural beliefs I've learned from my past. Then, I picture in my mind God's desire to give me abundant Life as a gift in His right hand extended to me with deep love and delight.

Again, I don't visualize what this looks like because I know that my natural thinking will get all wrapped up in the outcomes and results my flesh is counting on for Life. I literally visualize God's hand extended towards me with gifts that are beyond my ability to see and comprehend, but which will be wonderful and pleasant to me.

I intentionally lead my heart and emotions to long for *whatever* God choses to do for me, instead of what I would want Him to do through my own wisdom and natural desires.

And so, I go on with my day — *with Jesus* — focusing my heart on His Life-giving presence rather than on my circumstances. Even when trouble comes to me (which Jesus confirmed *will happen*), I immediately go to Jesus to receive His overcoming power and peace. I still have bad days — plenty of them! I still lose my focus on Jesus — we all do, and will continue to do so for the rest of our natural lives. I still get distracted with seeking better outcomes under the sun — often. But I've developed practices that quickly bring me back to the Life-giving reality of Jesus. I reminding myself of all the promises God has given me through His logos and rhema words. I intentionally *force* myself to believe in God more than my circumstances, because I've discovered that His desire is to bless those who do.

> *"He did all this so you would never say to yourself, 'I have achieved this wealth with my own strength and energy.'"*

Deuteronomy 8:17 (NLT)

ONE MORE THING

God wants to bless you with His presence, because it's His nature to do so. Jesus said He came down from the perfect comforts He had in heaven to give us Life — full and abundant Life. But God's ways to give us Life are not humanly understood. This makes the path to Life seem hidden to us. Therefore, there's *one more thing* we must do to find this elusive path. And without it, we will lose heart and fall away from the path that leads to Life.

CHAPTER 10

JESUS' SECRET: HOW TO RECEIVE THE GREAT GOOD GOD HAS FOR YOU

"...He rewards those who earnestly seek Him."

HEBREWS 11:6 (NIV)

God's core desire is to satisfy our core desires. *That's what He made us for.* He created us so we would experience His Life-giving abundance at all times. Even though mankind destroyed what God intended through sin, His desire to bless His creation still remains the same. That's why Jesus left the comforts of heaven to come down to our broken reality. He came to restore the Father's original creation intention. He said so in John 6:33 and 35 (NASB):

> *"For the bread of God is He who comes down out of heaven and gives life to the world." Jesus said to them, "I am the bread of life; he who comes to Me will not hunger, and he who believes in Me will never thirst."*

However, the singular human disconnect from this amazing promise is not sin, but unbelief. Our core problem is that we fundamentally don't believe He is the fulfillment of our desires — we don't believe Jesus is Life. Therefore, we seek other means to find happiness. Sin is what comes after our unbelief leads us to find Life in anything other than God. That's our sin problem. Jesus clarified this in no uncertain terms in John 16:9 (NLT):

"The world's sin is that it refuses to believe in me."

We're all seeking happiness every second of the day. This is true because God originally created us to live fully satisfied — we just can't help ourselves from seeking happiness. Blaise Pascal is my favorite French mathematician, physicist, inventor, philosopher, writer and Catholic theologian. He said:

"All men seek happiness. This is without exception. Whatever different means they employ, they all tend to this end ... [Humans] will never take the least step but to this object. This is the motive of every action of every man, even of those who hang themselves."

BLAISE PASCAL — Pensées (1670)

Our unbelief in the Life-giving reality of Jesus drives us to be desperately fixated on better outcomes and pleasant circumstances under the sun. Yet our fleshly efforts and strategies are missing the one thing that truly makes us happy — Jesus. Again, Blaise Pascal brilliantly confirms this reality:

"Happiness is neither within us, nor without us. It is in the union of ourselves with God."

So, here's the big idea of this last chapter. It's impossible to write enough books that will lead you to happiness in God — to abundant Life. There are simply too many variables at play that keep people from finding it. So, this last chapter reveals *the one thing* that will guarantee you will find what you desire. It's this: *you must seek God earnestly — more than anything else — with everything you've got!* Here's why this matters so much.

SEEKING EARNESTLY

Everyone is earnestly seeking happiness, every minute of their day. So, why did Jesus say few find it? The reason is found *in what* we are so earnestly seeking. Remember, God said, *"He rewards those who earnestly seek Him."* If we look at the dictionary, we see the word "earnestly" defined as:

> *"Serious in intention, purpose or effort; sincerely zealous; sincerity of feeling; demanding serious attention."* — Dictionary.com

My personal definition of the word "earnestly," which I believe aligns with God's requirement in Hebrews 11:6 where He said, *"He rewards those who earnestly seek Him"* is a mix of *eagerness* and *honesty.* Simply put, we must be *all in* with our belief that Jesus is the fulfillment of our desires — that He is abundant Life — even if we haven't yet experienced this heavenly reality. We must seek Jesus' promise of abundant Life with a ruthless and tireless eagerness. Otherwise, we will give up our search, and inevitably go back to seeking Lifeless outcomes under the sun. We just will.

However, eagerness is not enough. We must be *brutally honest* with ourselves and God throughout our journey of life. Just like the saying goes: "the path to Hell is paved with good intentions." Without an unshakable integrity to seek God and His ways, we will find ourselves among the multitudes Jesus said are upon the path to destruction. Consider this sad truth: *most of those who live their lives traveling the path to destruction believe they are on the path to Life.* Therefore, deeply humble and uncompromising honesty is required to avoid being fooled by our flesh, our emotions, and the devil.

SHAMELESS PERSISTENCE

But Jesus has a very unexpected requirement for those who want to be rewarded with the prize of abundant Life. It's found in a bizarre parable in the Gospel of Luke (one of my favorite passages in the Bible). Here's what Jesus said:

> *"Suppose you went to a friend's house at midnight, wanting to borrow three loaves of bread. You say to him, 'A friend of mine has just arrived for a visit, and I have nothing for him to eat.'*
>
> *"And suppose he calls out from his bedroom, 'Don't bother me. The door is locked for the night, and my family and I are all in bed. I can't help you.' But I tell you this — though he won't do it for friendship's sake, if you keep knocking long enough, he will get up and give you whatever you need **because of your shameless persistence."***

LUKE 11:5-8 (NLT)

It's hard to believe this is in the Bible, much less that it came from Jesus Himself! Here, Jesus analogizes God the Father as a person who is unwilling to get out of bed for a needy neighbor knocking at his door. Really? Is God bothered by our requests? Certainly not! The rest of the passage clues us in to what Jesus is showing us:

"And so I tell you, keep on asking, and you will receive what you ask for. Keep on seeking, and you will find. Keep on knocking, and the door will be opened to you. For everyone who asks, receives. Everyone who seeks, finds. And to everyone who knocks, the door will be opened.

"You fathers — if your children ask for a fish, do you give them a snake instead? Or if they ask for an egg, do you give them a scorpion? Of course not! So if you sinful people know how to give good gifts to your children, how much more will your heavenly Father give the Holy Spirit to those who ask him."

LUKE 11:9-13 (NLT)

Notice how passionately Jesus is telling us to seek, ask, and knock! He's revealing a secret here to receiving the desires of our heart. Jesus is declaring that *shameless persistence is required* to receive and find the great good God has for us. That's because our persistence reveals what we believe in the most — our circumstances, or God's Life-giving reality. Our shameless persistence towards God and His kingdom proves that we believe in Him as *the fulfillment and satisfaction of our very existence* above anything else. The intensity Jesus expresses in this teaching reveals how crucial our persistence is to receiving His gift of abundant Life.

However, don't miss the power of God's gift of the Holy Spirit offered at the end of this passage. It's easy to consider this gift like getting an Encyclopedia set for Christmas. Yeah, it's great for learning, but it's not what we desire as a gift. I've got be honest, the gift of the Holy Spirit at the end of all that "build up" did feel like a bit of a letdown to me too, when I first read this passage many years ago. Yet, I've discovered that without the Holy Spirit, we have **no** ability to find the abundant Life we so deeply long for. Without the Holy Spirit, it's an impossible endeavor. In fact, there are two massive benefits in the Holy Spirit to help us find the abundant Life Jesus has for us. Here's what they are:

Benefit #1: The Life-giving Spirit

The Holy Spirit is our guide to find true Life — no matter how broken our life may be. All the Holy Spirit does is lead us to abundant Life — that's His "job," His passion, and His desire! He never condemns. He knows us better than we do. And He's always *on call*, exclusively dedicated to lead us to all the good God has for us. If we leave the Holy Spirit out of our life because we don't understand how He works, then we will be leaving abundant Life out of our lives as a result! How's that for necessary? Here's what the Bible says about the life-giving work of the Holy Spirit.

> *"[Jesus] washed away our sins, giving us a new birth and new life through the Holy Spirit."*

Titus 3:5b (NLT)

> *"And because you belong to [Christ], the power of the life-giving Spirit has freed you from the power of sin that leads to death."*

Romans 8:2 (NLT)

> *"Shouldn't we expect far greater glory under the new way, now that the Holy Spirit is giving life?"*

2 Corinthians 3:8 (NLT)

Benefit #2: A God-sized counselor

Today people are all about having mentors, coaches, therapists, and counselors. I say *"Yes!"* to all the above! Why go it alone, when we can avoid making the mistakes others have already learned from? Why not gain the insight and knowledge of wise experts who are willing to teach and lead us? But in reality, all human mentors and counselors are just that — *human*. They're trying to find their way through life just like the rest of us. And most importantly, the path to Life is entirely unnatural to all of us. Therefore, it requires *supernatural insight and divine revelation* to find it. That's why Jesus sent us the Holy Spirit in the first place. Here's how important the Holy Spirit is in Jesus' view:

> *"But I tell you the truth, it is to your advantage that I go away; for if I do not go away, the Helper (meaning, the Holy Spirit) will not come to you; but if I go, I will send Him to you."*

JOHN 16:7 (NASB)

> *"But when He, the Spirit of truth, comes, He will guide you into all the truth … He will glorify Me because it is from Me that He will receive what He will make known to you."*

JOHN 16:13-14 (TNIV)

But there's more! The word for "Helper" in verse seven above — *Paracletos*, in the original Greek — has four powerful meanings which are incredibly beneficial to us. The Holy Spirit is *our comforter, our advocate, our intercessor, and one called alongside to help us.* Let me expand on each of these characteristics of God's supernatural gift to us:

1. **Our comforter:** We will have difficult times in life. Jesus made it clear we will have trouble and tribulation in this world. No one escapes adversity. However, the one He sent us has the ability to comfort us. We can ask Him for comfort any time we need some. He loves doing it, and it's His superpower!

2. **Our advocate:** We will grow faint in this quest, for it requires us to live beyond our natural ways. The Holy Spirit is our champion, supporter, defender, and protector. We can call upon Him in our moments of weakness to help us persevere.

3. **Our intercessor:** Our transformation will require many instances of supernatural intervention and grace. Anytime we encounter an obstacle we see no way of removing, or we encounter a problem for which we cannot imagine a solution, we must ask the Holy Spirit to intervene with God's power and wisdom. We must not operate in the realm of the natural, seeking our own solutions or outcomes. If we do, we will miss out on seeing God's miracles and divine appointments necessary for the journey. We must ask the Holy Spirit to intercede on our behalf to our loving and heavenly Father.

4. **One called alongside to help:** Because of the Holy Spirit, we are not on our own to figure things out. We must believe that Jesus sent us *exactly what we need*, and that He is at our side — on our side — to help us find the abundant Life Jesus said He came to give us. You're never alone in your Christian journey because the Holy Spirit is always with you, ready to help you.

The reward of shameless persistence is that God will *"give you whatever you need,"* as Jesus said in Luke 11:8, including a supernatural guide to help us find abundant Life! Shameless persistence only comes from complete and unshakeable belief that Jesus is the fulfillment of our desires even when we are in want. Shameless persistence is the only way to make it through the wilderness experiences we will face, and the only way to receive God's promised land of abundant Life on the other side. Anything less will rob us of the greatest reward we desire. Therefore, everything God created us for — to live a full and abundant Life — hangs in the balance. We must believe and seek this unseen reality *as if our life depends on it*, because it does!

> *"If God didn't hesitate to put everything on the line for us, embracing our condition and exposing himself to the worst by sending his own Son, is there anything else he wouldn't gladly and freely do for us?"*

ROMANS 8:32 (The Message)

> *"The seed is the word of God...[The seed that fell] on the rocky ground are the ones who receive the word with joy when they hear it, but they have no root. They believe for a while,* **but in the time of testing** *they fall away. The seed that fell among thorns stands for those who hear, but as they go on their way they are choked by life's worries, riches and pleasures, and they do not mature. But the seed on good soil stands for those with a noble and good heart, who hear the word, retain it, and by persevering produce a crop."*

LUKE 8:13-15 (NIV)

DAILY ALIGNMENT — OR DESTRUCTION

My car is a 4-wheel-drive SUV. If my car is out of alignment, this one issue creates discomfort and longterm costly damage. But I can still drive the car in that broken condition. The same goes for our lives. If we are not aligned with Jesus and His Life-giving presence on a daily basis, we will suffer discomfort and costly damage over the course of our lives. Adversity is the reminder that we must get aligned with Jesus, or else we will suffer far more loss and emptiness apart from Him than our own strengths and wisdom can ever secure. Remember, we have no life in ourselves — and neither does the world and its outcomes.

We must feed on the Bread of Life every day, or the hunger and thirst in our hearts will lead us further and further away from the abundant Life God created us to receive. Jesus promised this ultimate solution to our ultimate need 2,000 years ago — it's fully available for you right now — it's not a pipe dream!

> *Jesus said, "I am the Bread of Life. The person who aligns with me hungers no more and thirsts no more, ever."*

John 6:35 (The Message)

God's seven purposes that Moses revealed in Deuteronomy 8 are exactly what we all need to come to our senses about our condition here under the sun. They are the most loving thing our heavenly Father can do in order to reveal His Life-giving intentions for us, without violating our free will. Honest and repentant alignment with Jesus surrenders our will to His loving and healing presence. In due time, we will become increasingly transformed into people who begin to no longer hunger and thirst for worldly outcomes under the sun.

Rather, we will find an inexplicable contentment growing inside us, which is no longer bound to improved outcomes or pleasant circumstances. We will begin to live like few ever do. And because our heavenly Father is lavishly loving, He will bless us circumstantially in ways which will not feed and grow the inner beast of our flesh. His natural gifts will add to our Life-giving experience, rather than enable our naturally addictive ways.

Remember, there are only two paths to take in this life. The path of better outcomes acquired by our own strengths and wisdom leads to destruction, no matter how godly we are trying to live. I know. I've unknowingly lived on this path for most of my life. And everyone else on this path to destruction thinks it's the path that leads to Life. Every day, I still have to fight the natural urges and fleshly "muscle memories" that keep dragging me back to this Lifeless path.

The other path — the one that leads to abundant Life — is only found by fully surrendering our will and expectations to the indescribably good God who created us. To the degree we do so, we will receive the desires of our heart. However, we will experience intense opposition from the Enemy of our souls — and also from our flesh within us. Therefore, we must align ourselves with God and His heavenly realm — with shameless persistence — in order to find the path to Life.

If I don't align myself on a daily basis with the Life-giving presence of Jesus, I don't stand a chance to live the better way. Neither will you. No one does. So, I urge you to do anything and everything necessary to align your life, your will, your desires to the only Bread of Life, the only Spring of Living water, that is Jesus Christ our Lord. He revealed how vital this alignment is, when He lived our human reality:

> *"Abide in Me ... As the branch cannot bear fruit of itself unless it abides in the vine, so neither can you unless you abide in Me. ...* ***apart from Me you can do nothing.*** *If you abide in Me, and My [rhema] words abide in you, ask whatever you wish, and it will be done for you."*

John 15:4, 5 & 7 (NASB)

And so to close, dear friend, Jesus did everything necessary to make the path to Life available to us. It's now our responsibility to believe it, to seek it, and to fight for it. And so, as we come to the end of this journey together, I bless you in the name of Jesus to find what God made you for — to find full and abundant Life in His presence.

God bless you!

HEY!

THANKS SO MUCH FOR READING ME, BUT PLEASE DON'T LET ME DIE A LONELY DEATH ON YOUR BOOKSHELF!

Now that you're finished with me,
may I ask you for a favor:

KEEP ME FOR ANOTHER SNUGGLE!
If you're the type to read me again, we'll curl up again
with a hot cup of Joe and have more Quiet Times
together. I'll be here when you're ready. I can't wait!

GIVE ME AWAY!
BUT ... if you're not the type to read a book twice, that's
cool – I'll be OK. However please give me to someone
you know is in adversity. Pass me on to someone who
would be blessed by reading Mark's message. They
probably need me!

For so much more, visit:

www.HiddenPath.Life

Made in the USA
Columbia, SC
02 February 2022

55261324R00133